CW00725095

ON THE SEVEN

*For a complete list of Management Books 2000 titles,
visit our web-site on http://www.mb2000.com*

ON THE SEVENTH DAY

Ian Gouge

2000

For Sarah

Copyright © Ian Gouge 2001

All rights reserved. No part of this publication may be reproduced, stored in a retrieval system, or transmitted in any form or by any means, electronic, mechanical, photocopying, recording, or otherwise without the prior permission of the publishers.

First published in 2001 by Management Books 2000 Ltd
Cowcombe House
Cowcombe Hill
Chalford
Gloucestershire GL6 8HP
Tel. 01285 760 722
Fax. 01285 760 708
E-mail: mb2000@compuserve.com

Printed and bound in Great Britain by Biddles, Guildford

This book is sold subject to the condition that it shall not, by way of trade or otherwise, be lent, resold, hired out, or otherwise circulated without the publisher's prior consent in any form of binding or cover other than that in which it is published and without a similar condition including this condition being imposed upon the subsequent purchaser.

British Library Cataloguing in Publication Data is available
ISBN 1-85252-358-1

Contents

1

Introduction

From the Jaws of Certainty ...

Amid the many hundreds of aphorisms that exist in our rich and expansive language, few ring with the kind of solid truth that leads those who hear it to pause, nod and sagely agree. One simple maxim – that nothing is certain except Life, Death and Taxes – still resounds with absolute undeniability. Some years on, perhaps it might be acceptable to attempt an update, to modernise this somewhat definitive saying with a little contemporary hindsight.

"Nothing is certain except Life, Death and Taxes –
and that IT projects will fail."

Obviously this supplement cannot claim the absolute degree attached to either Life or Death; nor does it inherit that same air of undeniability that surrounds our inevitable battle against the omnipresent Tax Man. It does, however, possess a not insignificant ring of accuracy; echoes of dismal project experiences within the professional classes, supported by everyday problems such as inaccurate utility bills, undeserved letters of censure from financial establishments, and late, delayed or cancelled planes, boats and trains.

Despite everything that computer-based commercial systems now contribute to modern twenty-first century life, they have a general reputation akin to that probably earned by Jack the Ripper among nineteenth century physicians. To be frank, it isn't good.

Across the breadth of enterprises world-wide, this poor scorecard comes from decades of delay, lateness and high project costs. Ask any senior business manager for their view on computer systems and the majority of responses will be the same: at best "a necessary evil"; at worst a waste of money. And even those who give praise for System X or Application Y will be inclined to temper their assessment with some caveat, relating either to System X or the one it replaced.

Strange, is it not, that with years of experience behind the systems delivery industry, we should be faced with the same complaints that dogged the previous generation? Odd that despite the investment of billions of dollars into development methodologies, management training, and project scheduling tools, when project leaders proudly announce that their project was delivered 'on time and to budget' no-one believes them? Either that, or the suspicion is that somewhere along the line the project must have failed and its leader is simply attempting to deflect us from that fact by producing Gantt charts which no-one understands and figures that no-one can disprove.

The ultimate paradox in all of this is, of course, that in working with computers, we are dealing with simple Boolean logic; the certainty that the answer is either '1' or '0'. In tossing a coin, you would be reasonably hopeful that the result would fall either as 'head' or 'tail'. You would settle for nothing less. It is upon such a basic premise that all computer systems are formed.

Although this is an over-simplification of the problem, failure – at least in the theoretical sense – should not be an option. The path from Point A to Point B in any business application is inevitably more complex than switching a light on and off, or tossing a coin. The components may exist at that binary level, but the whole is made up of millions of such elements. Yet even so, the route through the system from Point A to Point B does ultimately submit to a version of the heads-or-tails scenario.

Given such a premise – and one which must be undeniably true until computers can think for themselves and therefore vary their response at will – it would seem reasonable to suggest that the systems themselves cannot fail; after all, they are simply doing what they are told. On this basis, the failure that dogs application system delivery must be introduced externally, outside of the technology. If we accept that any electronic hardware can fail from time to time –

like a video or washing machine – this then implies that it is the human element which is responsible for snatching defeat from the jaws of victory; and on the systems implementation route march, there are many opportunities for such an intervention.

Given that IT Project Managers starts out on each new quest with their sights firmly set on success, there is something tragic in this assertion. Largely, the ambition and desire to succeed is subversively – and unconsciously – usurped by an unseen and almost pathological drive to fail. An even greater irony is that often, out of that professional pride that pushes the Project Manager forwards, comes the deployment of the booby traps that will snare him later on; a damaging self-infliction arises quite unwittingly from his best intentions.

The desire to fulfil the contract between our business customers and ourselves (or even as a private, internalised pact to do a 'good job') leads us to commit to that which is neither possible nor practical. We do not mean to do so, but there it is. Optimism and the desire to please gives us the opportunity to wave goodbye to realism. Demands from the business can also lead us in this direction. Sometimes such pressures arise from the need to meet a very real commercial goal; often they are born from dissatisfaction. Whatever the source, the first rule for Project Managers must be to 'only promise what you know you can deliver'.

At the outset of any project, this means coldly and dispassionately recognising the demons of ambition and optimism and facing them down. So often IT projects are doomed within a few days of their launch when the Project Manager, fired-up by the prospect of having another chance to put together the 'perfect' project, gives his positive side full rein, thereby unleashing the devils that will stab him in the back later on.

Our business sponsors leave the project definition meeting or finish reading the project definition report hearing or seeing exactly what they want to hear or see; except for those who have been around the block before and know only too well what is likely to follow.

The question to be answered at this initial stage is a simple one: is it better to give the project's customers the promise we know they want, only to gradually disappoint them as time goes on; or is it better to manage all expectations up-front, and then deliver against the vast majority of the commitments subsequently made? We should start with the recognition that it will be people (both IT and business) who will bring failure to the enterprise, and act accordingly.

The purpose of this book is, therefore, to offer the Project Manager some guidance in terms of minimising failures. There are methodologies that will promise success if they are followed – and often the diligent Project Manager will find himself knee-deep in bureaucracy and administration with the project still falling about his ears. There are also general courses on management methods and techniques which submerge the Project Manager in highbrow intellectual theories – but when he gets back to the office, he invariably struggles to make them fit the job in hand and subsequently abandons his new toolset.

What I will endeavour to do here is to provide some guidance to better enable the delivery of successful IT projects in the 'real world'. Recognising that so much can go wrong even before the first program is written or the first data flow diagram is drawn, we will major not only on the commencement of projects, but also the stage before that; the definition of IT strategy.

Senior IT managers love defining strategy. Once they have 'risen above' the day-to-day nitty-gritty of 'doing' in an IT project environment, the route through management may lead them to the position where they will need to put together a medium- to long-term systems strategy, often for presentation at board level. Similar to any other project, the work relating to strategy definition is likely to suffer from those same gremlins associated with ambition and optimism – and the danger is that once a strategy based on unrealistic foundations has been accepted, then all subsequent projects spawned in its name will be handicapped before they start.

So, as we progress from strategy definition, through project planning and management, and on to execution, the book will be aimed at the practising Project Manager. Having said as much, I suggest that any senior business leader who is likely to be knighted with the rather dubious honour of 'Project Sponsor' would also benefit from a little 'inside knowledge'. After all, in an ever-more competitive business world, the metaphorical fans that systems' excrement occasionally hit seems to spread detritus in ever-wider directions.

If, at the end of this book, I have been able to offer at least one thing that will cut down the opportunity for failure just a little bit on that next project, then I will be happy. And please note, in following my own advice, I have diligently resisted the over-ambitious desire to tell you that 'read my book, and all your IT project problems will be solved, forever!'

A little bit of philosophy ...

Before setting foot on the path that is IT Strategy and Project Management (a path that is likely to boast its own version of the Tin Man and Cowardly Lion, by the way!), it is important that Project Managers establish their bearings. By this I mean that they should gain an appreciation of where they – and the applications and processes for which they are responsible – stand in the overall systems landscape.

In defining such a landscape, we can realistically divide the status of our general environment into a limited number of realms: Chaos, Order, Completion, and Simplification. Not only do these four elements represent a basic schematic to fit the systems world; they also flow one from the other, providing a broad route map for the Project Manager:

Chaos – The situation where the project (and in this case, 'project' can represent anything from a single application, the introduction of a new project administration regime, to defining an entire IT strategy) is out of control, without appropriate processes and controls to manage and steer it. Fundamentally the train is off the rails.

Order – Here management processes and controls do exist, and we are able to prioritise, order, and measure what is going on. This does not necessarily mean that we are doing the right thing, simply that we have some form of control over what we are doing.

Completion – The next logical step, in that the ordered project is now reaching its defined end-point and we are in delivery or implementation mode. Soon we will be able to draw a line under the project (whatever it might be) and take stock. In such an environment, it is likely that there will be a number of projects at various stages of completion at any one time. (Be wary, though! Very rarely does completion lead to drawing a clean line under anything. More often than not, project sign-off automatically leads to something else – such as the spawning of a maintenance project after the implementation of a new system.)

Simplification – Perhaps the only element where consideration of applications delivery strategy should come into focus. Our well-ordered IT world has succeeded in closing out on a number of initiatives, and, in order to move on, our goal should be to review what we have and initiate a number of new projects aimed at simplifying the landscape, i.e. to make it even easier to control and order – thus beginning the cycle again.

As Brown indicates, the Project Manager's job is to bring about change.

At the project level this can be seen in terms of new systems, business processes etc.; at the macro level, the shift from chaos to order and on to simplification.

As you can see, following the chaos-order-complete-simplify mantra offers the Project Manager a simple but effective means of quickly assessing the scenario in which he is being asked to work. The iterative flow from order to simplification – once you are out of chaos! – is logical, and one which will hopefully lead to an ever-more effective IT infrastructure.

However, one of the most basic mistakes made by IT management is to prepare new strategies and systems (i.e. aiming at elements of completion and simplification) whilst the general infrastructure is in a state of chaos. Without appropriate **control** – and, hopefully, the proof of an ability to successfully complete – burdening the existing IT framework with further complexities can only deepen the state of chaos; a surefire way of guaranteeing failure.

Knowing where you are on the systems chain gives you the opportunity to define a realistic initial goal; for example, if you are in chaos, you should ideally aim at order, nothing more. Keeping your sights on this short-term goal – with merely a glance at the longer term Nirvana of simplification – gives the Project Manager a chance of putting together something that will actually succeed.

One trend which, in the name of order and control, has proliferated in the recent past is the advent of the TLA – or 'Three Letter Acronym'. Once upon a time, coming up with imaginative names for applications was as creative as IT specialists ever got; after all, a career could be built around inventing catchy names for old first- and second-generation systems! However, as the IT world increased in complexity and began its interminable cycle of self-reinvention, more and more of its granular day-to-day elements began to demand appropriate labelling. I would suggest that part of the reason for this lemming-like charge – initially driven, albeit unwittingly, by hardware manufacturers – was that it gave IT Managers the comfort of an inner sense of control. If you could refer, with a degree of authority, to an 'ABC' or 'XYZ', this helped you to enhance an overall sense of managerial proficiency and well-being.

Not only is this sensation false, the worms have been out of this particular can for so long now that TLAs are of little use any more. There are three reasons for this. Firstly, they do not actually contribute anything in the drive to achieve control; secondly, those who use them often assume a 'universal understanding' which is both dangerous and unfortunate for anyone who comes into contact with them (particularly business users, who have enough trouble with 'techno-speak' as it is); and thirdly, there are so many of the little chaps wriggling about that many have duplicate meanings and are therefore doubly useless. What is a SAR? A 'System Amendment Request' or a 'System Architecture Requirement'? And is a PDR a 'Project Definition Report' or a 'Process Dataflow Repository'? You get the point.

So, a plea. Please try to avoid adding to an overstocked glossary already awash with these little uncontrollable creatures. Your business partners will thank you for it. For my part of the deal, I'll try and stick with English; TLA is my first – and last – TLA.

Abstaining from indulgence in this jingoistic party is not, of course, one of the critical things that will help you to minimise project failures. It may help communication – which is not, after all, a bad thing – but that is about as far as it goes. However, there are some maxims which, like the Ten Commandments, will hopefully help to keep you on the Yellow Brick Road. One – 'Only promise what you know you can deliver' – we have met already. This, along with the others we will encounter along the way are gathered together in the Appendices at the end of the book – where, by the way, you will not find a glossary of three letter acronyms!

The object of the Appendices is to offer a reference section on the ideas and notions contained within the book. In addition to the maxims, you will find some examples of templates referred to in the main body of the text. It might be useful at this point to clarify the role of the models and examples used in this book.

Firstly the models

Some methodologies and management theories present models much in the same vein as the overall treatise itself, i.e. they must be used as given, and are propounded as being 'right'. Project Management is not, of course, a science, and whilst the two-plus-two rule holds where it should, it is wrong to attempt to force management practices into any kind of mathematical straitjacket. Therefore, the purpose of any models offered here is merely illustrative; where used, they will be given to aid the visualisation of relationships between elements – such as time, resources, money etc. In the same way that I am not Sir Isaac Newton, these are not laws.

The examples

For my examples, I have invented a little cabal of businesses based around three industry sectors – manufacturing, retail, and financial services – and in each sector there is one large and one small enterprise:

Any example that bears resemblance to a real company facing a similar situation to that outlined is entirely co-incidental – either that or an uncanny example of the veracity that lies behind the principles of this work! Also, any persons depicted here are entirely fictitious, and similarity with actual individuals (living or dead) is entirely co-incidental. Having said that, let's face it – who hasn't come across the Mad Hatter or the Wicked Witch of the North at some point in their careers?

Finally, about technology ...

In much the same way as some Project Managers might look to a packaged methodology to hand them success, there will be those who calculate that by deploying a particular mix of technologies, they might banish the spectre of failure. A few years ago, for example, in some quarters there was a buzz that 'no-one who bought IBM ever got fired' – though this will not be one of my maxims!

Unsurprisingly, there is no magic formula – which is self-evident when one recognises exactly how fashion conscious the IT industry has become. Not only does it continue to recognise the big players on the systems' catwalk, it also plays homage to new concepts – even though these are often simply old concepts dressed up in newer rags. Thus in 1998 the train to catch was the Enterprise Resource Planning express leaving from track number nine; in 1999 perhaps you should have taken the 'e-commerce' bandwagon departing from platform twelve. Many of these fads are essentially old applications tarted-up – remember my comment about the industry re-inventing itself? As if to prove this assertion, already it appears that the Saviour-like qualities promised by Enterprise Resource Planning systems are beginning to wear off, and a new Messiah (perhaps 'Customer Relationship Management') is already waiting in the wings.

Where is technology going then? More to the point, should we worry? The problems relating to project failure are, as we have suggested, more about the management of technology than the technology itself. Is it not more important that you know how to plumb in and operate a washing machine rather than whether you buy a Hotpoint or a Zanussi?

For the IT practitioner – who has spent years growing up with technical things – ignoring the specifics of the technology when defining strategy (for example) can be particularly difficult. At this stage, knowing that you will need to deploy personal computers is enough – it does not matter if they are Dell or Compaq. You need to recognise the limitations imposed on you by your planning horizon, and the impact on any strategic plan of not only the fashion swings of the industry, but also the ever-increasing rate of technological change. More on both of these later.

So, forget the technology – Digital or Sun, the management principles will be the same. Yet even having said that, there will be some who demand a template: 'Microsoft', they will say, 'surely we should go with Microsoft? And IBM. And SAP.' Safety in numbers, perhaps. But not necessarily the right thing to deploy in your business. And remember, the industry is cyclical and innovative. Over the past few years, a number of the big players have been through a rough patch. Perhaps Apple is on the way back to a double-digit share of the desktop market, who knows? And two years ago, who would have forecast the impact of Linux?

Ninety percent plus of project failures will arise through an inability to manage the implementation of the technology, not the technology itself. If your methods are robust, if you have been able to impose order on your chaotic world, if your strategic direction and management tool kit are both sound, then these principles will apply across the board, whatever technology you choose to implement.

2

Principles

Exploding the myths ...

Before we consider the definition of IT strategy in detail, it is prudent that we should lay down a few ground rules; principles which not only apply in the rarefied atmosphere of strategic objective setting, but elsewhere as we progress through systems implementations. There are, of course, existing management concepts and IT project practices that the Project Manager may invariably – and sometimes, unquestioningly – use. Many of these will be sacred cows which have become enshrined in application development processes over the years – or which have been spawned to go hand-in-hand with modern systems thinking.

As we indicated on our journey through Part One, there can be no 'right' way, no single set of rules and processes for the Project Manager to follow and thereby guarantee success. The very dynamic of the environment within which today's IT professionals work means that simply because something worked on the last project – possibly one of our 'Sacred Cows' – this doesn't mean to say that it will work on the next. Much will remain valid, of course, but unless you start out on each new challenge with as open and pragmatic a mind as possible, almost certainly tricks will be missed.

If would be useful, would it not, to be able to provide a list of our old and well-loved cattle ultimately destined for the abattoir? Sadly this is not possible – the reasons being that very often sacred cows are particular to individual businesses, or IT organisations, or (dare I say it?)

IT managers themselves. When approaching any new project – be it strategy definition or legacy system maintenance – the manager brings baggage accumulated from projects past: those things that have been tried, tested and always worked; those things that were tried and failed. When the Project Manager sits behind the desk of his new project, what will he do? Almost invariably pull out the tried and tested, dust them down, and off he goes. This kind of initiation is quick and easy, and we're in familiar and comfortable territory almost immediately.

So, what's wrong with this? Well at first glance, not a lot. But let's say that old Project A was large scale and overseen by a steering committee which worked really well. If Project B is slightly smaller, less business critical, and focussed on a more limited group of users, then the steering committee is likely to be over-kill, top heavy and inefficient. Simply dusting the concept off and implementing it willy-nilly courts disaster.

Similarly if we were going from Project B to Project A, our inclination might be not to use a steering committee because on Project B it had been such a waste of time. In making this kind of value judgement, the Project Manager would be missing an opportunity to improve his chances of success.

This analysis – even using the simple example above – has two ramifications. The first is that a Project Manager's satchel of experience – his 'professional bag', if you will – is likely to contain a whole raft of tools, processes, ideas and procedures which, via a multiplicity of combinations, could probably handle most IT projects quite adequately. Therefore the message must be that all items are potentially valid for the next project – even those things that in the past were failures. So, empty your professional bag on the table and have a good rummage!

The second ramification is that, in accepting that our bag will undoubtedly contain some personal sacred cows, we might be tempted to argue that as their deployment should no longer be inevitable, perhaps they ought not be sacred after all. If this destabilising argument holds true, then by what creed does the Project Manager steer? In my view, the staff he leans on should comprise solid principles – such as 'only promise what you know you can deliver' – rather than more mechanistic tools. This approach has the added benefit of providing a professional set of mores that can apply across any project.

Take the mythical 'Life Cycle'. Survey a hundred Project Managers and I expect, for around 90% of those questioned, their first instinct would be to split any project into something akin to this:

1. Requirements Definition

2. Systems Design & Specification

3. Development / Installation

4. Systems Testing

5. User Acceptance

6. Live Running

Breakdowns such as this (including many subtle variations and derivatives) were born in the distant past when the system developer's primary tool was limited to something like COBOL. Without the availability of any sophisticated aids, and with IT still pretty much in its infancy, a structure such as this 'Development Life Cycle' came to be recognised as the de facto way of breaking down a project. Phases were progressed in a linear fashion; you started at the beginning, and – not surprisingly – finished at the end.

This kind of life cycle also provided the manager with a structure against which he could apply an estimating yardstick at the beginning of the project. A simple algorithm could be used to split the implementation effort into percentages by phase; for example, 15% on requirements definition, 10% on system specification and so on. Thus, with relatively little effort, planning and creative thought, projects could be kicked off with ballpark numbers in terms of effort, cost and timescale. Away we went! Perhaps this kind of inaccurate approach was one of the first catalysts for the poor reputation of systems implementations...

> ### WHAT CAN HAPPEN...
>
> "The Department wrote off costs of £41m, and acquired a replacement system ... at a cost of £6m." - Committee of Public Accounts on the Ministry of Defence's 'Project Trawlerman'. The need for a system was identified in the mid-1980s; a £32m fixed-price contract was agreed in July 1988 for an October 1991 delivery. The project was abandoned in November 1996 - over eight years after it began.

Whilst it can be argued the modern IT Project Manager is trying to achieve nothing different from his predecessors – and, therefore, that the simple life cycle structure still applies – it must be recognised that we have moved on. Modern development tools allow us to take other approaches to delivering systems solutions, with Prototyping and Rapid Application Development being the obvious examples. Tackling projects with these kinds of techniques (probably using CASE tools in many instances) effectively invalidates the rigidity of the old life cycle structure.

It would be foolhardy to dismiss totally the general process flow defined by the historical and monolithic approach, however. Some projects may benefit from being addressed in this fashion; many will not. Again, the prudent manager would be wise to extract all these development models from his bag of tricks at the beginning of each endeavour and weigh the pros and cons of each – rather than plumping for the one he knows best.

There is another fundamental reason for paying less homage to the mythical life cycle. Indeed, I have already indicated as much. Over the past few years, it has been recognised that the root cause of many IT projects' failure is in initiation – at that very point where we divided our world into 15%, 10%, 25% and so on. Taking a simple model – and ducking the real preparation and planning tasks – will no longer suffice. Neither will the deployment of an arbitrary estimating model.

Rules of thumb can be still be a useful mechanism for Project

Managers to check the results of their detailed initiation work, however. If, for example, experience tells you that the development effort 'feels' like 20% of the project, but your rule of thumb suggests that you should be planning to put around 35% of your resource there, it might be wise to revisit those estimates and assumptions that gave you the 20% in the first place.

Thus there may still be a place for the Development Life Cycle and the kinds of rules of thumb that accompanied it; however, as the bedrock for successful IT implementations, they have been outgrown. Again, rather than deploying these kinds of sacred cows – which only work on a limited range of projects – we need to recognise a set of principles which give us a chance of success across all projects. Instead of staking our careers on little more than circumstantial evidence – 15%, 25%, 20% etc. – we need to see if we can get a little closer to the truth.

How not to stumble out of the blocks

Given the recent emphasis by IT project management theories on the way projects are initiated, it would be prudent to consider a small number of significant elements related to the start-up process. Again, these observations will apply equally to kicking-off a multi-million dollar global package implementation through to a simple Visual Basic application on a local intranet – though with obvious allowances made for scale!

The first and often most fundamental problem is a critical management imbalance which can jeopardise any undertaking. I am referring to the situation often faced by the Project Manager in terms of responsibility and authority. It would not, I believe, be fanciful to suggest that in at least 90% of IT projects, the Project Manager has the responsibility to deliver, but without the authority which increase his chances of success.

What do we mean by this? In simple terms, once we have been through the definition and acceptance of the strategic proposal or the system implementation plan, the Project Manager's contract gives him the task of delivering against a defined programme – normally live running of a system or systems – within the framework of the definition report or plan which has been produced in support of that programme. In addition to defining 'X' – that which is to be delivered – the Project Manager is also given two further elements: 'Y', the timescale; and 'Z', the budget (effectively this means both money and resource).

X ... the agreed result
Y ... the timescale
Z ... the budget

Let us assume that the Project Manager is happy agreeing to all three, and he believes that given 'Z' he can deliver 'X' within the time proposed, 'Y'. Of these three elements, it is only 'X' and 'Z' over which he can have any control: time will pass whatever he does, and he cannot buy more of it; all he can aim to do is to achieve as much as possible within any given period. Unfortunately – and this is where the imbalance comes into the picture – the Project Manager, given responsibility for 'X' is very rarely given overall authority to effect delivery of it, i.e. he has no real control over project resources, 'Z'.

Let me suggest some tangible manifestations of the result of a Project Manager not being given the authority to deliver that for which he is being held responsible:

Scenario A   Realising that there is more work than estimated, the Project Manager calculates that with two extra staff he can, with prudent manipulation of his project budget, still deliver 'X' within both 'Y' and 'Z' (the famous 'within Time and Budget' statement!).

(Outcome A)   Staff numbers are controlled by Human Resources, and they veto any proposal to increase headcount. Often this may include temporary resources too.

Scenario B   The Project Manager recognises that he is not getting enough dedicated User Resource input into his project. Requirements are likely to be poorly defined and he despairs over the likely depth of User Acceptance Testing before going live. His need, therefore, is to be able to allocate specific users to certain elements of the project in order to better guarantee success.

(Outcome B)   User resources are obviously managed elsewhere. The

Project Manager is told that they are too busy to be freed up for systems development work – which is an IT project after all!

Scenario C

In order to provide the most effective development environment for the project, the manager knows that some additional hardware – file servers, PCs etc. – would be beneficial. Whilst a significant amount, he can manage the cost within his budget.

(Outcome C)

In the first instance, based on the company's defined authorisation thresholds, the Project Manager does not have the authority to spend the kind of money he is looking at. Secondly, any capital expenditure of this kind needs to go to a separate committee for approval – perhaps made up of other Project Managers as well as senior members of the business community, the former often being less than supportive as they try and promote their own projects. Or even more simply, the purse strings are held by someone who does not understand IT projects and is unable to see the need for 'additional' hardware spend.

I could go on. This situation – being judged on delivery, but being hampered en route to that delivery – is all too common. Where does this stem from, and what can be done about it?

Perhaps this imbalance arises as a result of a lack of trust which may, in turn, be driven by a host of things, many of them political: a poor delivery record in the past; an innate mistrust of systems people by the business; an unwillingness to give up control of real expense dollars; senior business managers protecting their own turf, and so on. Whatever the cause, the Project Manager can be placed in an invidious position.

So what can he do? There are some steps that can be taken during the project initiation phase that may help if not to resolve such issues before they arise, at least to raise awareness of them. I would suggest that the following questions are explicitly asked, with the answers clearly documented in any Project Initiation Report.

? What is the Project Manager's individual authority limit in terms of spending before needing referral elsewhere?

? In the event of needing to exceed that limit, what is the process – and who are the people – involved in agreeing the spend?

? What is the Project Manager's individual authority in terms of sanctioning additional resource before needing referral elsewhere?

? In the event of needing to exceed that authority, what is the process – and who are the people – involved in agreeing additional resource?

? What is the Project Manager's individual authority in terms of co-opting additional business resource onto the project before needing referral elsewhere?

? In the event of needing to exceed that authority, what is the process – and who are the people – involved in agreeing business resource?

? What is the Project Manager's individual authority in terms of adjusting any of the deliverable dates as defined at the outset of the project before needing referral elsewhere?

? In the event of needing to exceed that authority, what is the process – and who are the people – involved in adjusting the plan?

The answers to each of these questions will have some potential impact on the project and the ability of the Project Manager to satisfy his three key variables: the size, quality or scope of his deliverable, 'X'; his ability to meet the agreed target date, 'Y'; the likelihood of meeting both 'X' and 'Y' within the budget given, 'Z'. But even asking these questions is, as we shall argue below, not enough.

Typical within documents that define most significant projects in the modern systems environment are sections that refer to 'Assumptions' and 'Constraints'. Very often there is some confusion as to the apparent overlap between these, and here we shall consider what they are – and how they are misused or under-utilised. Before doing so, however, it is worth reiterating that no matter where you consider the most appropriate location to formalise these kinds of project parameters (including the answers to the questions above) the most important thing is that they are documented somewhere and that this document is seen and signed-up to by the business leaders of the project.

Assumptions and constraints

We might define an 'assumption' as those significant elements within a project that its manager is assuming will be present or available. By 'constraints', we mean those things that will hinder the successful completion of the project in accordance with the defined goals, targets etc. Overlap is most evident when one considers things like resource provision:

➡ **Assumption:** 'That the resources required to execute tasks as defined in the plan will be available.'

➡ **Constraint:** 'Lack of resources to execute tasks as defined in the plan will impact on the delivery schedule and quality of the final solution.'

Similarities are obvious; where considerations such as these are located – in either or both sections – is a fundamentally matter of preference for the individual Project Manager. Again, the emphasis must be that they are clearly documented somewhere.

The problem with the assumptions and constraints statements as predominately used in Project Definition Reports is that the manager who drafts them assumes, naively, that in converting his concerns into black and white he is somehow protecting himself. This is plainly wrong. When a project is going off the rails, the Project Manager who points back to a statement which implies 'told you so', is likely to be asked why, if he foresaw the issue arising, he failed to do anything about it. There are two messages here: firstly, use statements of assumptions and constraints dynamically, or do not bother with them at all; and secondly, make them meaningful tools to help you manage the project, rather than feeble strands in a gossamer safety net.

What do I mean by this? Whether we choose to phrase our concerns as either Assumption or Constraint, at the end of the day we are referring to either something happening or not happening. In simple physics, every action forces some kind of reaction – and there is no reason why our Project Definition Report should choose to disobey the laws of physics. Thus, if we state that we assume 'that the resources required to execute tasks as defined in the plan will be made available', in the event of this assumption being proved false we need to state a) the impact this will have on the project, and b) what we will do about it. Without such clarity, the bland statement 'that the resources required to execute tasks as defined in the plan will be made available' will be meaningless to any Project Sponsor or Steering Committee. Is the following not better?

Assumption: That the resources required to execute tasks as defined in the plan will be made available.

Implication: Failure to resource the project at the appropriate level is likely to result in either/both a delay to the delivery date of the project and degradation in the quality of the delivered system.

Action: In the event of a reduction in project resourcing below the planned level – and failing to secure the resource needed – the Project Manager will re-schedule the project by either extending the delivery date or reducing the scope of that which is to be delivered.

Obviously, the wording will vary according to the individual Project Manager's taste, but the message is clear: do not simply point out the areas of potential concern and compromise, but be specific in terms of the likely impact, and be explicit about what you will do. In the example above, you must say that you will re-plan the project. No ifs, buts or maybes; you will do it. You are making a clear statement that you intend to execute your responsibility as Project Manager.

Having gone this far, you still need to go one step further. You need to ensure that your assumptions and constraints remain dynamic. With this in mind, you need to state how you will manage them. Typical would be a brief but regular review – certainly no less frequently than monthly – at which all stated assumptions and constraints could be tested (and even new ones added). If a need for action was identified, what this action would be has – if we follow the suggestion above – already been clearly defined and communicated. More importantly, assuming that the definition report has been agreed by the business, any action the Project Manager needs to take has, to some extent, been endorsed in advance.

This approach of using assumptions and constraints dynamically and as a true management tool is all about the Project Manager effectively exercising his responsibility. It is about being **proactive.** More importantly, it is about establishing and maintaining control over that which it is within our power and remit to control.

Obviously, any form of Initiation or Project Definition Report will be key in setting out the framework for the project ahead. (See Appendix B for sample contents of a Project Definition Report.) It should, if well executed, give all major players in the project – both IT and business – a clear view of what is intended to be achieved. More importantly for the Project Manager, it should also be a clear statement as to the boundaries of his responsibility, a definition of his perceived authority (and the authority of others), and a guide as to how the project will be managed.

Given the importance that this kind of management tool represents, it is perhaps unfortunate that – in ignoring our first project management maxim – the document might also be responsible for providing many of the manager's coffin nails later on. Very often the Project Manager takes significant time and trouble to produce a Project Definition Report that appears to be a quality document. He likes it, and his users like it. Everything in the garden is, as they say, rosy; and there are smiles in abundance as the death warrant is signed. A good initiation document should help towards guaranteeing project success, but so often it does not. Why? A few suggestions:

a) Enthusiasm leads the Project Manager to promise things that cannot be achieved, i.e. the promise to deliver too much, the promise to deliver too quickly, the promise to deliver too cheaply – often all three!

b) Factual statements upon which the significant parameters of time and money are based have been arrived at through inadequate or inaccurate calculation and preparation.

c) The real impact of stated assumptions and constraints has not been considered, clearly pointed out, or remedial action identified.

d) By not being honest with himself, the Project Manager has chosen to duck difficult issues and failed to tackle them up-front.

e) Similarly, in order to impress, the Project Manager has committed to a management regime – weekly Issue Log reviews, detailed time reporting etc. – which he cannot possibly maintain.

f) A catch-all, but one or more significant factors that should be considered at this stage and included in the document have been missed out completely.

There is a maxim in motor sport that suggests that, when taking a corner, 'save a tenth of a second on the way in, gain a second on the way out'. With the Project Definition Report – the foundation of the work ahead – something similar must surely apply; 'a day well-spent in preparation, saves a week in execution'.

> *'Planning is an investment to save time later.'*
>
> Trevor Young

Facing facts

When the Project Manager finds himself sitting in front of the blank sheet of paper that represents the beginning of either the Grand Strategy he has been asked to outline, or that competition-busting package implementation, there are a number of incontrovertible requirements that he must address. Of these the two most obvious elements – and those which fundamentally define his role in the overall scheme of things – are the definition of what is to be delivered, and the plan that will enable that delivery. Without a clear statement of 'what?' and 'when?' – and, in accompaniment, 'how?' and 'at what cost?' – failure, probably in multiple forms, is bound to follow.

In addressing the general issue of planning first, I do so with the assumption that the goals and objectives which await satisfaction – by either the broad strategy or the individual project – have already been suitably defined, agreed and documented. In part three of this book, we consider the definition process in more detail; for now, however, I want to consider general aspects of planning that pertain as much to the grand plan as the individual system implementation.

Many years ago, I worked on a project where, quite rightly, a great deal of time and effort was invested at initiation time. Project management tools were still in their infancy, but were already proving a significant boon to leaders of projects as they attempted to map out their route to success. After a considerable period in planning mode – weeks, rather than days – the Project Manager emerged from his PC, plan in hand. It was January – and with an astonishingly blissful degree of certainty, he felt able to tell me what I would be doing on the morning of November the 11th!

A good plan is, without doubt, one of the keys to success at either strategic – or project – level. The Project Manager is most unlikely to be able to 'win' without a plan – and by 'win' I mean sell his strategy or implementation programme to those who (a) must 'buy' it, and (b) then recognise that he has been successful in its delivery. However – and this was the failing of the 11th of November Man – the plan must be realistic; it must be appropriate and fit the need. Did I end up doing what had been forecast for that mid-November morning? I doubt it. The rest of the team and I were probably already out of line by the end of February, and come Autumn we were probably on version six of the 'master plan'!

How, therefore, should the Project Manager balance the need for a plan with the appropriate degree of realism in foresight? The answer is **Horizon Planning.**

An analogy – if you were to undertake a drive across Europe from the north of France to Athens, taking in various sights and cities along the way, how would you plan it? Firstly, you would probably sit down and broadly map out your route, identifying the major highways that would occupy the bulk of your journey. You might then identify the places you would like to visit – major cities or sights of particular interest, some perhaps off the beaten track – and putting these two elements together, you might then sketch out an itinerary which would allow you to pre-book your hotels along the way. Sound reasonable? Would your next step then be to dig out a street map of Verona and plan in detail your route between motorway and museum – a journey you might not be taking for another three weeks? I don't think so – unless you were like our 11th of November Man, of course! In all probability you would have the detail of your first day well defined, from the moment your wheels touched the continent to your head touching the pillow. Day two would dawn, another day's route would be drawn up, and away you'd go. Horizon planning! You know roughly where you will be in three weeks – but you know exactly where you are going today.

For the Project Manager, the key to horizon planning is to recognise the 'distance' to your next horizon: it might be two months, or the end of a phase of a large project; perhaps it will be the end of the financial year, or some other business-related boundary. In any event, your parameters will not be Europeans cities, miles, or hotels, but projects, deliverables, budgets and the like. Only time remains as the consistent factor. Perhaps your strategy has six key elements to be tackled in sequence; do these represent your planing horizons? Or are you undertaking a project that has four major phases? Again, horizons may simply fall out. If they do not, and if there is no significant business driver which imposes any timeline boundary on you, then draw your horizons at no greater than quarterly intervals, if not shorter. (Indeed, for departmental managers, I would suggest quarterly horizon planning has other major benefits that we will identify in Part Three.)

With the notion of horizon planning, goes hand-in-hand the concept of the **rolling plan,** moving forward (as our motorists would have) chunk-by-chunk until successfully delivering on our project(s) – or a trans-European motoring holiday!

'Aim for successive rounds of practical results.'

Tom Peters

This notion of a rolling plan, based on the horizon model, is one that has a number of important implications:

➡ a manageable, time-bound, and well-defined **planning frame** – no 11th of November!

➡ an efficient **concentration of planning effort** at the beginning of each period – time is spent on the period ahead, not that still a year away

➡ **natural checkpoints** for major or long-term strategies or projects – if business plans change, effecting managed change to IT plans is easier

➡ increased **manageability** over resources – this includes greater control over both money (budget) and people

➡ **Improvement in focus** with respect to deliverables contained in the plan – concentration only on that which is due to be delivered next, which consequently, if well-managed, will lead to an improvement in productivity and general morale.

This last point leads us back to that second fundamental of the Project Manager's overall remit, namely definition of that which is to be delivered. Broadly, as we have already suggested, this may already be known: a company-wide SAP implementation; a new web-based e-commerce system; a major upgrade to the payroll package; or a re-configuring of the network infrastructure. There will, almost certainly, be one 'big thing' at which the Project Manager is aiming – and, if the manager concerned happens to be responsible for the entire IT shooting match, then these are likely to be many and various. Such large scale deliverables are, however, not only insufficient when allied to a plan, horizon or otherwise – they are also profoundly undermining of planning in general.

If you have a plan, how will you measure progress against it? Our European holiday-makers would know they were in trouble if, on Wednesday, they were scheduled to be in Berlin but still hadn't made it across the French-German border. They wouldn't wait until the end of their three-week holiday to know they were in trouble. So why should you? 'Live running of System X' may be fine as a goal three months hence, but it simply will not do in terms of a planning or tracking aid.

'How is progress?' the Finance Director asks.

'Fine,' you reply with a smile.

'On schedule?'

'On schedule!' you assert.

What happens when he then says, 'Prove it!'? All the charts, reports and diagrams in the word will not – or should not – satisfy him. You need evidence. Think about how progress can really be measured and proven. Will it be according to the number of work days spent on Project A or B? Will it be your estimate that you are still 3% under the projected budget? Really?!

Progress can only truly be measured by delivery – by being in Berlin when you said you would be. That is (a) delivery against the plan – the 'when' and 'at what cost' – and (b) the delivery of something concrete – the 'what'. Any plan – no matter what its duration, scope or timescale – can only be worthwhile if it specifies real concrete deliverables along the way. The Project Definition Report on May 4th; the revised System Specification on June 10th; the draft Strategic Plan on February 9th; the prototype web site on October 23rd. These are concrete things. You can see and touch them. You can tell if you have made a promised delivery because you were aiming at something physical and you have the tangible evidence of its existence. Being thirty-five percent through the development of your strategic plan is meaningless; but producing an Invitation to Tender, an Organisational Resource Plan, or whatever, proves progress. And if you have delivered these concrete 'things' when you said you would, what more evidence can you provide?

Planning for the concrete gives the Project Manager more than the ability able to prove to his boss – and himself! – that he and the team are actually doing something. It enhances his overall ability to control, and in more than one way. If you force yourself to include concrete deliverables throughout your plan at a reasonable frequency – perhaps two or three a month, per project – then there is a good chance that the process of defining these deliverables will help improve the quality of your plan, i.e. concentrating on the concrete may assist in areas such as identifying gaps in the plan, or exposing weaknesses in the plan's logic. It also enables members of the project's team to be clear in terms of what is expected of them, assisting in motivation, and providing a useful aid in individual performance measurement and skill-set development.

Aim to deliver regularly, and aim to deliver 'real things'. Not only is this a solid maxim for planning, but it also provides a very real opportunity to increase the credibility of your project, strategy or department.

Quality and documentation

There are two other aspects in this area which the Project Manager needs to consider up-front, namely quality and documentation. For different reasons, each of these is seldom considered at the outset of any project:

> **quality**, because it is 'difficult' and the Project Manager often naively assumes that there will not be a 'quality problem'
>
> **documentation**, because systems people hate producing it!

Defining any kind of 'Quality Plan' is tricky, but affirmation of a quality product – whatever it might be – should be a fundamental element of any project's overall goal. Indeed, the nature of the core business within which the IT manager has to deliver his systems may have a significant impact on the degree of quality required in any delivery; and by 'quality', we mean characteristics such as accuracy, reliability, clarity, speed, efficiency and so on. For a financial services organisation, a quality application is most likely one which, above all else, guarantees the integrity of data and the accurate processing of that same data. In a manufacturing company it is likely to be the provision of systems which deliver minutely accurate technical instructions to production machines, or which calculate unerringly efficient production schedules.

WHAT CAN HAPPEN...

The National Insurance Recording System

Live with 'over 1500 unresolved system problems ...'
Committee of Public Accounts

For a Project Manager, however, the consideration of quality is not simply about the end product; it is about ensuring the quality of all those deliverables along the way. It is not inconceivable that at the end of a project, an application is delivered to production (to time and budget, of course!) which meets all quality checks set for it – however it is not exactly the application users wanted. The reason? There was a flaw in the Project Definition Report – a mistaken assumption, or a poorly worded objective – which went unnoticed, thereby leading to the wrong product being delivered. Such an oversight could have been weeded out with the appropriate quality check. In the case of key documents, for example, the adoption of a formal inspection process – a thorough, multi-party review of the report for clarity, ambiguity etc. – might well have saved the day.

Unless the utmost degree of quality is demanded by the business – pursuit of the mythical 'Total Quality' – as with planning, identifying any quality management process for a project will be down to defining appropriate depth and realism. One approach is to identify all quality management options, then cost them out – usually in terms of both human effort and elapsed time. Once this has been done, these could then be prioritised and the most important added to the plan. And these quality tasks must be added to the plan, up front – otherwise they simply will not get done.

Examples of quality management tasks:

- formal inspection on key documents
- ensuring some form of process flow diagram is produced by any developer before they start 'coding'
- having these process flow diagrams 'walked through'
- producing a detailed unit test plan, and getting this signed off before testing begins
- scheduling project audits (more of this later) ... and so on.

WHAT CAN HAPPEN...

The London Ambulance Service's automated allocation system, designed to tackle response time and resource relation issues

1987- first attempt; 1990 - abandoned (£7.5m); February 1991 - relaunch; January 1992 - partial system; November 1992 - system crashes and is closed down, leading to manual operation. There were organisational changes in April 1991, October 1991; and a reorganisation in 1992.

Of course, modern application development tools – and the trend towards system engineers, where traditional programming and analysis skills are combined – actually leads us away from many of the above. Rapid prototyping, fast development turnaround, and the generally increased pace of the systems world must mean – somewhat paradoxically – a reduction in the quality of the end product. A PC-based application may look sexy, colourful and fun to use, but quality may have suffered.

Whatever approach is taken to quality – and there must be elements of quality management in any plan – this should be documented in any strategy statement or project definition report: what quality steps will be in place – and what steps have been considered, but left out. Make no mistake, the latter will represent a risk to the project in some shape or form.

Early consideration of documentation issues has much in common with quality management: it is typically seen as an unwelcome distraction, and often ignored completely. But, like instilling a credible quality regime, appropriate addressing of documentation issues can both improve the end product and assist in providing the Project Manager with those concrete deliverables along the way.

Obviously, there are two aspects to documentation: 'internal', systems-related documentation, and 'external', user-related. Looking at the internal first, we have already suggested some examples when looking at quality – namely a test plan and process flow diagram. There are obviously multitudinous others relating to all systems aspects, from network infrastructure diagrams, through operating procedures, to application-related elements. If, for example, you are instigating a new procedure for your help desk staff with respect to handling and logging calls, then make a document defining that procedure a concrete deliverable. Inspect it with your users too. That way you satisfy both the need for concrete deliverables and improve the quality of what you are doing.

User documentation is harder, for two reasons: firstly because much of this will relate to business process rather than system execution, and secondly because IT people – as technicians – tend not to be very good at producing quality user documentation. There are a number of feasible approaches depending on the nature of the project, such as:

- employ a specialist technical author
- co-opt users to produce the supporting documentation themselves
- get IT team members to include it as part of their delivery
- don't produce any, and rely on limited on-screen, context-sensitive help.

As with any quality programme, the best approach to documentation is to define the options, cost them out, then choose what is to be included and the approach to be taken. Document this, and state what will not be done; again there may be some limited risks attached. Also, the key must is to be brutally realistic: know your users and audience, and try to understand how they work. How many projects have wasted considerable time and money producing glossy, seven-volume user manuals that sit unused on Users' shelves? Too many.

More myths

A few years ago, undoubtedly as one of the precursors to Total Quality Management, a brief fad spread through the systems world suggesting that the only viable goal – and particularly in application development – should be 'zero errors'. Whilst this may be a laudable aim, as with so many myths it is singularly unachievable, particularly in a technical environment which grows ever more complex. Even if a Project Manager, embarking on a new project, applies a comprehensive quality management regimen and includes all the possible checks and balances at his disposal, there will still be problems.

In as much as things like quality and documentation require early consideration, there must be recognition that errors will occur, and in doing so the clear understanding that these will need to be catered for. Of course, how 'errors' are defined will be something of a moot point: failure of a developer to understand a specification and in consequence deliver inappropriate function, is one example. Perhaps another might be the installation of inappropriately powered network file servers – despite all calculations made in advance.

The utilisation of a reasonable (i.e. practical and pragmatic) quality management system will help reduce errors. However, when these do occur, they will require managing, as errors – effectively unexpected events that require additional effort to correct – will cost, certainly human effort, and possibly cash pounds as well. For this reason, an error management programme should be included in all types of project, and as with our consideration of quality, the execution of that programme needs to be documented in advance – if only to (a) prove to any project sponsors that you know what you're doing, and (b) to get acceptance of any (marginal) costs of such prudent action.

One of the major reasons the zero-error notion lost prevalence was the ascendancy of new development tools that came with fourth generation languages, and in particular software that offered some degree or other of **Computer Aided Software Engineering** (also known as CASE tools). Moving away from an environment where every facet of an application needed to be hand-coded (using something like COBOL), increasing reliance became placed upon automated development tools which were bound to improve the quality of the finished product – weren't they?!

> Leintz & Rea's assertion that 'the approach of using Java and other similar tools ... makes systems management easier' is incorrect. Development and maintenance might be easier, but management could actually be compromised in such an environment.

As we have already suggested, despite this change of tool set, there has been no meaningful shift in the fundamental purpose of systems delivery, and hence no profound change in the problems faced by Project Managers. If the tools are more dynamic (in all senses of the word) the broad goals have remained static; i.e. the delivery of computerised 'systems' designed to meet specific business needs. It might be argued that in some respects deliverables have changed somewhat too, but the key management issues remain. It may be Visual Basic rather than COBOL, or a relational database rather than indexed sequential files, yet despite the fads and fashions of the technical environment, the principles suggested here remain valid simply because they apply to the management process and not the technical environment.

> Lientz & Rea suggest that the notion 'to be successful, projects require dedicated resources' is a myth. This may be true; however it must also be recognised that the provision of dedicated resources will increase the chances of success.

Currently one of the most popular and resilient aspects of recent systems fashion relates more to management approach than specific technological advance, though it does to a large extent depend on modern development tools. I refer to **Rapid Application Development.** This is the notion that application systems can be developed in a more responsive and dynamic way by the use of small, dedicated, mixed IT and user teams, working in a fast prototyping environment within a defined 'time box'.

Such an approach is widely touted, and many organisations will profess to 'doing RAD', as if in making such a statement they have found a panacea for all their systems ills. Do not be fooled; and do not undertake Rapid Application Development unless all the necessary rules can be adhered too – particular those relating to the provision of a full-time, dedicated, mixed-discipline team.

Proponents of such a rigorous 'time-boxed' approach might well suggest that there is little room for quality programmes and documentation on their project. Indeed, they may even suggest that there is scarcely room for any planning whatsoever!

In the purest incarnation of Rapid Application Development, they might well be right, and are able to point to fast, innovative systems that have been delivered through some kind of 'seat of the pants' methodology. If your organisation is able to make the necessary commitment to Rapid Application Development that it truly demands, then why not try it? However, it is entirely possible that management overhead and bureaucracy might actually increase rather than decrease as a result.

In the vast majority of cases – and the business, not IT, will tend to dictate here – true Rapid Application Development will not be possible. What will be possible however, using the principles outlined above – such as horizon planning and a focus on regular and meaningful, quality-checked deliverables – is a management method that should provide a comparable degree of controlled dynamism.

The human factor

Many years ago when I was first appointed to the lofty heights of project management (as opposed to team leadership), I recall asking my new boss what I was now expected to do.

'Do?' he said quizzically, 'You don't 'do' anything.'

Naturally, I protested. After a number of years as an enthusiastic and successful 'doer', to be told that particular skill would no longer be required came as something as a blow.

'You'll see what I mean ...' and thus ended – somewhat cryptically – my new job definition.

After several months, it became clear what he had been driving at. Instead of the low-level doing I had been used to – the coding, the analysis, the testing etc. – my new job involved becoming a politician and an enabler. It became my function to create the environment in which other people 'did'; my charge was now to manage and control.

Crossing this particular Rubicon is particularly difficult for technical people in two distinct ways: firstly, it means letting go of much of the day-to-day 'hands on' work experience to which they have become used; and secondly, it involves suddenly becoming a planner, diplomat and people manager – an entirely different set of skills to those which enabled the rise towards the top of the pile in the first place. If anything, it is this latter, 'fish-out-of-water' experience which forces many good IT technicians to become poor managers – and perhaps another small contribution towards IT's less than brilliant reputation with some business people.

Of all of these new skills demanded of senior IT managers, adapting to the people management aspect is probably the hardest task. All too often, for example, the old doer surfaces as the manager, considers an approach taken by one of his team, and cries, 'That's not how I would have done it!' Indeed, many managers, in refusing to let go, like to keep their hands dirty – a well-intentioned meddling which can often lead to unfortunate outcomes both in terms of team morale and flawed deliverables!

From a realm where his focus was honed by a blinkered vision – on this program or that test suite – the manager has now to face the demands of supervision. The very word – 'super' 'vision' – suggests a broad overseeing which is both new and difficult; and often it is a challenge the ex-technician fails. I mention it here simply to offer a possible solution to senior managers' responsible for entire departments or very large projects. In the same way one might consider employing a technical author to handle the bulk of documentation issues, why not take on a professional 'super-vision-ist' to focus on personnel-related aspects? More likely to be a human resources professional than an ex-programmer, such an individual might very well offer an effective means of assisting the senior manager in handling those personnel matters which are critical to being successful.

The resource conundrum that the project or senior manager will not be able to delegate is that relating to organisational shape: exactly how should the departmental or project team actually look? Considerations such as roles and responsibilities will be examined in Part Three when we look at organising the project, but for now we restrict ourselves to the getting of resources.

Before the manager can go and recruit his team – from whatever source, internal or external – he needs to have an established view on a number of factors:

➔ team size
➔ management structure: hierarchical, flat or matrix
➔ organisation chart, including broad definition of all roles (at least titles, if nothing else!)
➔ likely 'layers' of management – the management distance between 'top' and 'bottom'

Perhaps some of these will be predefined by the way the organisation as a whole works, or by a given budget (either financial or in terms of headcount). Above all, however, the manager needs to have a firm grasp on the goals and objectives ahead, and these need to be something he is committed too, believes in and is able to sell. Nothing gets people on-board as readily as a supervisor's enthusiasm for the job in hand and the proposition he is selling.

> *'The importance of a project is (far) less conclusive*
> *in determining its success than the level of commitment*
> *of its initiator(s)'*
>
> Tom Peters

Ignoring for the moment internal business resources, there are broadly speaking two types of technical resource available to the manager – permanent and contract – and the mix of these may well be critical to the success of the project in both short- and long-term. If, for example, a technical specialist – perhaps a database administrator – is hired for the six months of an application development project, what happens at the end of that period when the specialist leaves? The ideal may be to have an internal resource ready to take over. Succession planning such as this must be considered from the outset as the implication may be the need for an 'extra', effectively non-productive body to be on the team for the last two months of this period to give him the chance to gain the necessary skills and experience. If considerations such as this are ignored, the manager may find both himself and his project suddenly compromised.

Whatever the shape of the organisation, at some point there is likely to be the need to look for resource outside the company. The Human Resources Department may well have procedures and rules laid down for such searches. Large companies might handle all recruitment directly – including the placing of advertisements etc. The majority will rely, in some shape or form, on recruitment agencies. Of these, there are probably too many to count in the field of IT personnel, and the danger the Project Manager must avoid lies in asking a large number to resolve the same recruitment problem. If he does so, then he will quickly find himself in the land of diminishing returns, swamped by dozens of curricula vitae, and pestered by innumerable phone calls.

So, some suggestions:

- Have a very short list of agencies with whom you have worked or are happy to work. One or more may be specialist, but there really should be no more than three or four.

- For each vacancy, offer it initially to one agency and give them a couple of weeks (if you have the time!) to respond; then consider broadening the net. Always provide a summary of mandatory requirements.

- Be clear in terms of your expectations: the number of curricula vitae you will consider for each post (which forces the agency to do the filtering for you); the terms you are happy with; the general service you expect. Never forget you are in a buyer's market when it comes to recruitment services!

A good, responsive agency that delivers the kind of quality candidates you need and works in a way that suits you can be worth its weight in gold. If any let you down, then do not be afraid to relegate them to the second division and give someone else the chance to step up to the oche.

As suggested above, contract resources may represent a double-edged sword: you buy-in expertise to meet a specific need; that resource then gains significant experience of your systems and the business practices they are designed to support; they then leave, taking all that experience with them – and all at an inflated cost to you! Not a particularly pretty picture is it? However, the external resource may bring experience that cannot be found internally – on that new Enterprise Resource Planning system, for example – and they may be your only chance to get a running start from day one.

The Project Manager, in defining the shape of his organisation, getting a handle on the resources already available to him, and with the project plan in mind, needs to define up-front where the gaps are that need filling, and how he will do so. Is instant skill required, or can he afford to go through a recruit-and-train programme? Much will depend on the criticality of the position, and the duration of the project – not forgetting, of course, the impact of external consultants on that already stretched budget! Whatever resource map he comes up with needs to be documented just like the quality management and error management programmes as there is bound to be an impact on timescales and budget. All too often, delays in getting the right people on board at the right time leads to slippage in the project.

And finally a word about that scare business resource. The first question to be addressed is 'do you need dedicated resources from the business community?' – e.g. do you 'do RAD'? If the answer is 'yes', then your approach should be the same as for your technical resources: define what you need, then go and get it – though your peers and the personnel department will almost certainly be your source, rather than an external body. You will know, of course, even before this stage, whether or not such a request is likely to succeed. If part-time resource is either adequate or all you are going to get, then I suggest the following:

1. Identify the skills and business experience needed (by 'position').
2. Identify the likely demand on their time – when and how much.
3. Draw up a short list – in preferred sequence – of those business personnel you would consider suitable (always more than one per post).
4. Enter the negotiation battle!
5. Once you have commitment from line managers in the business, formalise it.

> *'Projects normally operate outside the normal routine*
> *of business life.'*
>
> Sunny and Kim Baker

(But projects are the norm within IT. Is it any wonder then that there is often a culture clash between the two?)

It is entirely likely that you will not get your number-one choice every time – and possibly not to the level of commitment you need either. Again, if this is likely to pose any kind of risk to your endeavour, extend the timescales or impact quality, then document it in your strategy plan or project definition document; if you need to adjust plans, do so.

Lastly, one of the most useful tactics available to the IT manager is to cultivate an informal network amongst business colleagues. By this I mean not only supporters within the senior echelons, but among the most effective and competent of the junior ranks. There will always be the guy in finance who knows his stuff, is highly PC literate and bright as a button. Recruit him as an ally. Encourage the informal 'can I just run something past you ...' Such an approach will boost his self-esteem, and give your function informal access to a knowledgeable and willing resource.

Pain now or pain later ...

Before moving on to consider definition of IT strategy, we need to turn our attention to a final collection of issues which the Project

Manager is undoubtedly likely to face at some point or another. In addition to further elements for 'up-front' consideration (see how important initiation has become!) there is one key imperative which is all too common.

Let us assume that the Project Manager has diligently drawn up his plan or strategy, taking into consideration all those elements suggested in this book. He has a detailed route map of where he wants to get to and how he intends to get there, and proceeds to make a quality professional presentation to his business sponsors. Whilst they may appreciate the quality of his work and are very enthusiastic as to his proposed delivery, they have some bad news: either it is too expensive, or it needs too many resources, or it will take too long to implement.

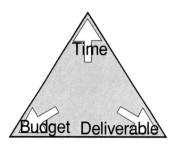

Often, the balancing act faced by the Project Manager is seen as a triangle with budget, time and deliverable at its points. There are variations in this model where the apex 'deliverable' is replaced by 'quality' etc. In my view it would be better to consider the triangle as representing the whole of that which is to be delivered, with each apex as one of the fundamental elements needed to ensure that delivery, thus:

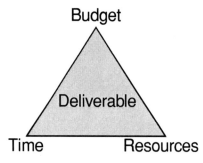

In this way it is easier for us to see the effect of any insistence that there should be a limit on one of the three elements concerned: i.e. the area within the triangle (that which can be delivered) is reduced. Given such a scenario, the Project Manager has two options: he must either (a) compensate by attempting to increase one of the other variables, thereby returning the triangle to its original area (though in a different shape – and this may be significant in itself); or (b) he must reduce the scope of what he is to deliver. To do neither invites almost certain failure.

Of course this corrective action will sometimes be unacceptable or impossible, and the Project Manager will be faced with making cuts in this plan – probably in the areas of quality, documentation, error correction, training etc. – with a proportionate, if not exponential increase in risk. Occasionally, despite all his best efforts, he will be faced with what appears to be an impossible project.

The kinds of circumstance highlighted above re-enforce the importance of a clear strategy or project definition document at initiation time, outlining what is to be delivered and the three key parameters in the triangle. Such a document is not only sound and professional practice, but it is ultimately good for the business too. In exercising his responsibility, the Project Manager must do all that he can to ensure he protects the business from mistaken assumptions and poorly informed decisions.

Scope of what is contained within the triangle is obviously critical, not only in terms of the objectives – such as implementation of the SAP R3 package, for example – but also with respect to the ongoing impact of such a delivery. It is not uncommon for an application development project to omit any reference to subsequent maintenance of the delivered system, or for a web-based e-commerce solution to ignore the impact on the local network infrastructure, communications bandwidth utilisation, and so on. It is important that focus is given to such considerations at the outset; this becomes a necessity if maintenance implications are to be factored in to the overall plan. If not, then I would contend that it is still important to address them early, outline future impact, and propose a continuous solution.

For example, it may be suggested that by implementing a new accounting package in the place of bespoke software, the number of

IT resources required to support the new software would fall by 50%. Such a claim might indeed form part of the project justification in the first instance. What if, once the package had gone live, it was found that this was not the case, and at least as many people as before were needed in the IT function?

There is a critical situation here with respect to implementing package solutions, and one which is continually growing in impact as the software – and the environment it runs on – becomes increasingly complex. Take this scenario:

Year 1

January	Package A goes live running against Database B, utilising PC system software C, and a network architecture based on D
June	An upgrade to Package A is announced, providing additional e-commerce functionality
August	A future release of the PC system software C is forecast

Year 2

February	You install the upgrade to Package A (a four month project) only to find that it performs badly on the existing infrastructure
April	The network infrastructure is upgraded to address performance issues, still with the existing version of D
July	The PC software C is now available and is rolled out
September	Again an upgrade of the infrastructure is needed, this time with a new version of the architecture software, D

Year 3

February	An upgrade to the database B is announced to take advantage of the new power of the latest releases of both C and D....

Sound familiar? And we said we would need fewer staff! Obviously there is little a manager can do with respect to the industry giants who make such moves, but he can recognise the potential impact and try to identify what this would really mean to the business.

In terms of managing package software, he can actually do much more. Let us assume that in deciding to take Package A, the users request a small modification, thereby taking the software away from its 'vanilla' form. You are asked to provide a quote as to the effort required for this change, and calculate that it will take five work days – say around £2000. 'Bargain!' thinks the business, 'we'll have a few more' – and at the end of the day perhaps there are fifteen changes totalling something like 75 work days. Okay? Most definitely not!

One of the biggest mistakes made in this area lies in the estimating of changes to package software. When, in the February of Year 2, you come to install the next version of package A, will it be straight forward? No, because you now have those fifteen modifications to deal with. Not only must they be re-coded into the new version of the software, they must be re-tested too; and not simply the modifications themselves, but the impact of the changes on any new function provided in the base package. Thus the original 5 days is now inflated to cater for an extra 2 days re-coding and 2 days re-testing. Your 5 has become 9; nearly twice the price. And consider the knock-on effect of multiple changes, banging against each other. It is not impossible for what should be a simple software upgrade to cost as much as the initial implementation.

Assuming a package implementation of 1000 days, with each of 15 modifications 'costing' 5 work days, a simple chart will help illustrate the potential real cost in terms of 'knock-on complexity'.

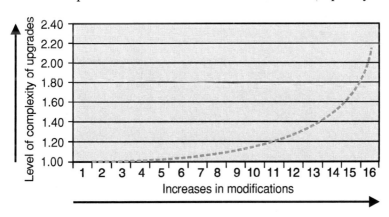

As can be seen here, from a datum level of complexity – '1.00', where we have vanilla software installed – the inclusion of bespoke modifications gradually pushes this figure up to where an upgrade of the software would be over twice as complex as it might otherwise have been. This makes the original 75 day estimate woefully inadequate over time – especially if the subsequent 'vanilla' 200 work day upgrade requires over 430 work days.

Whilst the co-efficient used to calculate these 'future costs' of modifications will vary from package to package, it is critical that the Project Manager attempt some form of quantification at the very outset of such a project to ensure that the true costs of moving from vanilla to raspberry ripple is understood. Indeed, such considerations might well influence package selection at the very outset of a project.

In the example below, we consider two comparable packages: the first, with the better business fit, is considerably more expensive than the second, which can deliver the same functionality (after modification) at a lower base cost. The instinct is to choose the latter – until we look at the impact of those changes on our first upgrade... (NB: days are charged at £400, and the cost of reapplying the modifications at upgrade time is taken as half the original effort, multiplied by the complexity factor.)

	Cost	Modifi-cations	Days	Implement-ation cost	Upgrade cost	Reapply mods. (days)	Com-plexity	Extra cost	Revised cycle	Overall cost
Package A	£50,000	4	20	£58,000	£5,000	10	1.1	£4,400	£9,400	£67,400
Package B	£15,000	15	75	£45,000	£1,500	37.5	2.2	£33,600	£35,160	£80,160

Obviously these numbers are illustrative only, and the 'complexity multiplier' would need to be arrived at for each individual circumstance, but they do show the potentially significant impact of making multiple modifications to package software. If there's really a message, then it's 'don't do it'!

And finally two elements of broad IT management that are rarely considered at planning stage:

➜ managing the exposure to technological redundancy
➜ disaster recovery.

Of the two, the latter is probably the least sexy element of any strategic plan or project implementation schedule, yet it remains a key responsibility of the Project Manager in his assurance of uninterrupted availability of critical business systems.

Most IT sites will have a disaster recovery plan in place in one form or another, usually covering provision of emergency hardware support at the primary business location. Remote site recovery may also be catered for, hopefully as part of a reasonably comprehensive business recovery plan, i.e. not something that is just confined to the systems department. Many projects will, at first blush, have little or no impact on the existing disaster recovery plan; more significantly, it is entirely unlikely that any potential impact will actually have been considered. Yet any project which adds new software or hardware to the infrastructure, or expands demand on existing capacity must, by implication, generate some knock-on effect with respect to the disaster recovery plan. For example:

- More powerful PCs are now being used; are these covered in the off-site plan?

- An e-commerce application has lead to an increase in routers and other network elements; is this capacity covered via the emergency trailer contract?

- A new, 'global' enterprise resource planning implementation is going live; does the disaster recovery plan not only cover the new system in the UK, but consider requirements in Europe and beyond?

The approach in this area should be three-fold:

1. **Define** what can go wrong
2. **Check** existing contracts and plans to see if you are covered.
3. If not covered, **plan and cost out** what additional backup will be required.

Any necessary improvements to the disaster recovery regime come, therefore, as a direct result of implementation of a strategy and/or project(s), and in consequence should be catered for as part of that project. Of course it may be that appropriate enhancements are covered outside of the implementation project budget, but that is merely a matter of administration; the important thing is that the need is recognised. If many things can go wrong, then at least some of them will – so it must be prudent to try and get them covered.

'Delays in implementing projects place them at risk of being overtaken by technological change.'

Committee of Public Accounts

Similarly, it is all too easy to focus on the immediate priority and forget about the future; after all, you cannot see beyond the end of this year's SAP implementation, and after that there's another two years of the strategic plan to go. This may be true, but in more than any other field, technology is evolving so fast, it is difficult to keep pace with. Recognising this is not enough, however, for two reasons. Firstly, some of your competitors will be getting several steps ahead of you – which is bad for the business – and secondly, some of your more technically able users – the hobbyists! – will do likewise. How do you respond when, for example, a senior user comes to you asking questions about a technology you haven't even had time to touch – like embedding images from a digital or video camera into PowerPoint presentations and sending the finished article on CD-ROMs to the sales force? What does that do as far as perception and reputation is concerned?

It may be a luxury that apparently you can ill afford, but surely it would be prudent to include an element of research and development in that strategic plan? After all, it may be that some new and peripheral technological advances could offer very real business benefit at relatively limited cost. You might argue that this actually forces inclusion of R & D in any overall strategy or long-term project due to speed of change in the industry – this, and that there will always be newer and better (faster, cheaper) ways to do the same things.

3

Strategy

I have a dream ...

Asking senior IT managers to define a 'strategy' is akin to letting a little boy loose in a free toy shop! IT people love setting strategies – unfortunately they often approach them as if they were a giant train set, and before you know where you are, investment has been made in something that might look quite nice but simply goes round and round in circles without really getting anywhere.

There is also a danger of that flavour of superiority and arrogance peculiar to IT folk suddenly surfacing. This was perhaps most prevalent in the early days of commercial computing when technical staff saw their salaries rise out of all proportion to their business colleagues, and with it the adoption of the, 'I know what's best for you when it comes to computers!' approach. Hopefully this is less in evidence today – but watch out for, 'Strategy? Okay, okay – my territory. Move out of the way!'

Being asked to define a strategy is not an excuse for that pet project you've always wanted to have a go at, nor – and this is more common I suspect – that massive SAP or Oracle implementation that will look good on your curriculum vitae and be easy to sell to the business as a cure-all. Very rarely is the strategist offered carte blanche, nor should he be. Any IT strategy worth its salt must deliver benefit to the business – and significant benefit too, as strategy often equates to big bucks.

'A coherent strategic vision, fully informed by a detailed understanding of the future needs of the organisation, is an essential starting point for strategic planning, which in turn provides a basis for the realisation of the vision.'

Stephen Flowers

So the key must be to understand the goal – even in the most broad of terms – and this goal must be driven by the needs of the business. Sorry ...

The first question must therefore be, 'What are we really trying to achieve?' – and must be asked of, and defined by, the business. Hopefully there will be a business plan available as a jumping off point:

- Expand the business in Germany to increase orders significantly within three years, by x%.
- Reduce the cost of manufacturing all end products by y%.
- Cut headcount in all business support areas by z%.
- Improve the speed of servicing customer orders ... and so on.

Often the business plan will cover a three or five year period – so wouldn't it be nice if we tied the IT strategy in with that? As they stand, the examples above are of use to us in terms of the general direction of the business, and understanding that IT can be a partner in each; more work is needed to break out (a) an overall strategy to support them, and (b) a series of tactical projects aimed at delivering against that strategy.

One critical mistake often made at this point is in setting the scope for the desired business improvements. You can only set the target for German sales, manufacturing costs, headcount, and speed of service if you know what they are now. If you already have 50% of the German market for example, a target of doubling orders would probably be over-ambitious to say the least! It is important that this clarity exists to ensure that realistic objectives and challenges are taken on by the business; because if these are unrealistic, there is a pretty good chance the IT team will be asked to deliver the impossible!

Additionally, any strategic plan should include some internal, IT-specific goals – and be as specifically quantified – in addition to those falling out from the business plan. Perhaps there is a need to replace all desktop PCs with laptops, or to improve the resilience of the local area network. Whatever it might be, it is important that these sit alongside the business goals, are couched in the same terms, and subject to the same kinds of justification. Improving the systems environment must be advantageous to the business if it better enables IT to deliver against business-related goals.

'A key aspect of retaining the support of the organisation
is to ensure that the objectives of the project coincide
with the business objectives of the organisation.'

Mark Brown

If this is so at the project level, how much more important is it for the strategic plan?!

So, in defining the strategy, it is vital to know:

(a) where the business is now
(b) where we want to get to
(c) the contribution IT is to make.

Once we have a defined end-point, the roadmap can be drawn up; without an explicit goal, how will we know where we're going – or even if we do, when we will have got there? Let's consider one of the examples above: 'Cut headcount in all business support areas'.

Where are we now?	Where do we want to be?	Possible IT goal to support objective
Finance - 18 staff	Reduction of 2	Reduce month-end processing time by upgrading existing acounting software
Secretarial - 12 staff	Reduction of 1	Provide a private secretarial network to allow sharing of workload
Personnel - 7 staff	Reduction of 1	Implement new integrated personnel and payroll system
Information technology - 13 staff	Reduction of 1	Improve network and desktop infrastructure to reduce support overheads
Total - 50 staff	Reduction of 5	

Obviously, as they are quoted above, the IT goals are inadequate and imperfectly defined, but the example does illustrate how one can begin to pull together IT threads from a business plan. Also it should be stressed that the finance, personnel and secretarial functions themselves will need to make changes – probably procedural – in support of the overall business goal. These should ideally be noted in the IT strategic plan in order to emphasise – where relevant – that the IT objective is part of a range of measures aimed at delivering benefit and that it may be driven or impacted by changes elsewhere.

'The implementation of an IT system is not an end in itself.'
Committee of Public Accounts

It should also be recognised that there can be both 'good' and 'bad' strategies – and more often than not, any overall strategic plan will unfortunately prove to be a combination of both. This is not to say that the individual initiatives proposed therein are necessarily flawed or impossible to achieve, but rather that they may be less than valid in a particular business environment – even though it appears that they address a defined business need. Additionally, strategies can be viewed as suspect when (a) they are purely IT-driven, (b) there is no business strategy behind them, or (c) no clear end-point has been defined.

Let us consider a small group of companies who have all expressed the same business goal, and the elements of an IT strategy that has been proposed.

The Companies

Auto Partz Ltd. are a high-volume supplier to the car industry (mainly UK, but some distribution in Europe) with a modest investment in IT systems.

Gnomes 'r' Us are specialist reseller of imported ornaments, with a very limited systems capability.

Big Bucks Inc. is a global financial services organisation with a massive investment in IT, both UK and Internationally.

The Goal

To improve the efficiency of the order processing cycle to enable:

a) direct order entry by customers (target 10% of orders within 2 years)

b) faster turnaround of order-to-shipment (average reduction of 25% within two years)

c) improved order-to-invoice processing (50% reduction in incorrect invoices and a decrease in average time to send invoices from 5 days to 3 days, both within one year)

The Strategic Plan

➔ **Option 1** – implementation of a web-based application to enable the remote placing of orders directly into the core system.

➔ **Option 2** – implementation of a company-wide enterprise resource planning package.

➔ **Option 3** – interim enhancement of existing core systems to facilitate orders placed through traditional electronic data interchange methods.

➔ **Option 4** – provision of laptops with a bespoke PC order entry system and e-mail connectivity.

The Outcome?

Auto Partz' customers are limited in number, but are large organisations – such as Ford and Vauxhall – who can generally be regarded as sophisticated users of IT within their own companies. With this in mind – and given the fact that we are talking high-volume supply/orders – Option 3 immediately stands out as a viable choice. Whether or not this is to be an interim solution will depend on the status of the existing core systems. Implementation of such electronic ordering is likely to benefit the customer too. This move would help address all three business goals to various degrees. It would also be suitable for non-UK customers. Option 1 would seem less suitable given the customer profile, and Option 4 irrelevant. Option 2 would only be a valid proposition in support of the final two goals if (a) the existing systems were failing, (b) it addressed additional goals and (c) the business could justify a significant increase in IT spend.

For **Gnomes 'r' Us**, the customer base is very different, being made up of Garden Centres, a few supermarkets, smaller hardware retailers and individual members of the public. Taking this into account – and given the scale of IT investment within the company itself – Options 1 and 4 are the best choice; they are relatively low-cost and low-risk, and the combination should offer an improved service to the majority of the company's customers. Again, some positive impact could be seen against all three goals. Option 3 is a non-starter as too few of the company's customers would themselves have the facilities to trade electronically; and Option 2 is in a completely different financial and systems league!

Big Bucks Inc. represents another situation altogether, particularly in that the company processes vast amounts of data on a daily basis and is critically dependent upon the quality of that data. Unlike the previous two companies, Big Bucks' major concern may well be the last goal – 'shipment', for example, being much less critical. If there are problems with existing systems, then Option 2 – implementing the relevant financial modules from something like SAP or JDEdwards ('One World' enterprise resource planning solution) – may well be a solid proposition. All the remaining options do have validity depending on the mix of customers and the time it will take to implement a new corporate system. Being a global organisation, taking on Option 2 may also allow the company to offer a homogenous solution world-wide.

In summary:

	Auto Partz Ltd			Gnomes 'r' Us			Big Bucks Inc.		
	a	b	c	a	b	c	a	b	c
Strategy 1	✓	✓	✓	✓✓✓	✓✓	✓✓	✓✓	✓	✓
Strategy 2	?	?	?	✗	✗	✗	✗	✓	✓✓✓
Strategy 3	✓✓✓	✓✓	✓✓	✗	✗	✗	✓	✓	✓
Strategy 4	✗	✗	✗	✗	✓✓	✓✓	✗	✓	✓

Whilst this is a relatively simplified example, it does illustrate how four perfectly sound strategic IT objectives, each aiming a identical goals, can be 'good' or 'bad' depending on the business environment in which they exist. Undertaking any of the strategic tasks in the situation where a '**×**' is shown in the summary chart above provides examples of where the strategy would be flawed either because (a) it was IT-driven, or (b) as there was actually no truly viable and relevant business strategy behind it.

In each case, of course, there needs to be a detailed assessment of the impact of the strategic proposals. It is not enough to simply say that Option 1 will assist with Goal A; the strategic plan will need to make an assessment of the eventual impact in terms that can be measured. After all, in addressing our Budget-Resource-Time triangle, we are defining the cost of the strategy in specific terms; if a project is late or over-budget – in terms of both money and resource – we will know, i.e. effectively the area of the triangle defined by their presence can be measured. In some way or another, there must exist another triangle behind the one representing the cost of implementation, this second representing the benefits to be gained from the project by the business.

This side of the equation is most often neglected, and in two radically different ways. Firstly, the benefit case is usually cobbled together by the IT person responsible for producing the strategy without research into the 'now' of the business area to be effected by his initiative, and with broad numbers being plucked from thin air and manipulated into giving him a decent cost-benefit case. Who has not seen something akin to this:

System Implementation Costs:	Hardware	£250,000
	Software	£300,000
	Resources	£750,000
	Sundry	£150,000
	Project Cost	**£1,450,000**

System Benefits:	Increase in Orders of 2% (pa)	£475,000
	Warehouse efficiency gain 1% (pa)	£125,000
	Raw Materials savings 5% (pa)	£625,000
	Administration Efficiencies 2% (pa)	£65,000
	Project Benefit (pa)	**£1,290,000**

According to these figures, the project pays for itself in Year 2, and from then on you are 'quids in'. Apart from the immediately obvious omission of on-going maintenance costs, key questions need to be asked about the stated benefits. Firstly, whose estimates are these, i.e. where have the numbers come from? And secondly, in what form will the benefit accrue, i.e. fewer staff, reduced inventory, increased profit? A larger number of organisations that one would imagine – or hope! – might be inclined to accept a project based on the numbers above, only to find that at the end of the development period, and into Year 2, they had spent probably nearly two million without any tangible proof that it had been money well spent.

> *'Key decisions on IT systems are, therefore, business decisions, not technical ones, and should involve senior management.'*
>
> Committee of Public Accounts

With strategic elements such as these, it is vital that the business 'buys in'; not only in terms of defining the 'now' position, but also in estimating benefits to be gained, i.e. only people from the business community can give these numbers credibility. More than this however, someone – or in the case of our example, probably four people – need to be given the responsibility for delivering those benefits. This is our second area of neglect. The senior IT manager can only be responsible for delivering his side of the deal; such strategic goals are a partnership and must carry shared accountability for their success. Who has not heard of a situation where IT has been blamed for a failure of a system to deliver the benefits promised? This shared ownership helps in many ways, key of which are:

➜ to get business buy-in to significant IT projects

➜ to ensure not only a return on investment, but overall business improvement, i.e. a greater chance of delivering against the strategic business plan.

The key message is that IT projects are ultimately – and need to be recognised as – business initiatives, and the responsibility for their success (in terms of both cost and benefit) is a shared accountability.

Remember the compass

Having considered some of the general issues that can befall elements of any strategy – the importance of the business plan; 'good' and 'bad' initiatives; projects that have poorly defined benefits without committed ownership – we can return to consideration of how to put the strategy together.

Once complete, the IT strategy should represent a blueprint for success – not only for the IT function, but for the business too. As such, we need to ensure that the framework within which the strategy operates offers as solid a foundation as possible. In saying this, we mean that a number of things need to be clearly defined before setting pen to paper:

→ the terrain within which the strategy is to operate
→ general expectations with respect to the strategy
→ the question of scale
→ management and ownership.

Obviously the IT strategy is not defined in isolation; it should be driven by – and gain credibility through – the business it is designed to support. Because of this, it is important that the strategist begins by gaining an understanding of the geography within which he is working. In many respects this involves appreciation of business culture, business ambition, and the current status of the IT function – both in terms of systems and reputation – within the community it supports. Some simple examples:

? Is the business particularly traditional and conservative? If so, beware the overtly radical and dynamic.

? Are you working in a fast-passed, rapidly developing business sector? The three-year, mega-project may be totally unsuitable.

? Is the business growing and if so, through organic growth or acquisition? If acquisitive, a flexible approach to smooth the take-on of new organisations will be key.

? Does the existing IT function have a poor reputation? Look for small projects to deliver business benefit quickly, as well as those to improve existing systems.

In as much as it behoves the IT Manager to understand these aspects of the 'terrain', it is also important that he attempts to manage expectations of all parties – including himself – in terms of (a) what the strategy will contain, and (b) if implemented successfully, what it will deliver or enable. It would be foolhardy, for example, to allow any in the business community to think that, within a certain period, all existing problems associated with any particular functional area would magically disappear if this were patently not the case.

Perhaps one of the most important factors is knowing where the IT function sits in relation to the Chaos-Order-Completion-Simplification model as discussed in Part One. Your location on this systems' cycle will have a significant bearing on the balance of your strategy. Indeed, the following matrix suggests the kind of influence this starting point can have on your proposal.

	Timescale	Existing systems	New Developments	New Technologies
Chaos	1 year	❖ Significant remedial programme ❖ Control and Quality improvements	❖ Limited to small-scale, low-cost, quick wins ❖ Curb adding function to existing systems	❖ Should be avoided at all costs
Order	2 years	❖ Standard maintenance programme ❖ Software upgrades to existing systems	❖ Consideration of new business applications, e.g. e-commerce/web customer relationships data, e-commerce/web	❖ Look at low-impact, non-global systems, e.g. laptops, group-ware
Completion	3 years	❖ Reduction in enhancement of current systems	❖ Major upgrades or replacement of individual systems	❖ Further enhancement of and 'leading edge' systems
Simplification	3 years +	❖ Development freeze on systems to be replaced	❖ New corporate solutions, replacing multiple systems	❖ Significant research and development activity

Whilst the examples in this matrix have focussed on business applications, a similar chart could be drawn up to cover hardware, desktop productivity software, personal computers, network infrastructure etc. It is important to notice how, as the strategy grows in terms of duration and is being built on decent foundations, the weight of effort – and therefore expectation – shifts towards the right-hand column. This is indicative of the effect your 'starting position' can have on the strategy, and it is important that the business community is made aware of this. Undoubtedly, there will be occasions where either the business plan or business pressure indicates that major systems replacement or new corporate solutions are wanted – but if you are currently in a chaotic state, such an approach is fraught with difficulty and risk.

In as much as we have a notional triangle to represent the major constraints of project delivery – and hence the overall 'size' of what is to be delivered – so we might consider something similar for our strategy as the key factors of **time, budget** and **resource** are equally likely to be in evidence. This is not unreasonable given that a strategy represents a collection of projects drawn together by a consistent vision and direction. It is important, therefore, that the manager responsible for drawing up the strategy has an appreciation of the general scale within which he is working.

Many factors will help in gaining an idea of where these boundaries should be drawn:

Time:
- current place in the Chaos-to-Simplify cycle (as above)
- scope of the overall business plan, i.e. 3- or 5-year
- other business imperatives e.g. take-overs, divestments, acquisitions etc.
- status of existing projects or initiatives e.g. perhaps there is 18 months left on an SAP roll-out.

Budget:
- last year's spend – obviously!
- general financial targets for the business, e.g. expansive or reining back, looking for savings
- profitability and its relation to investment i.e. is n% of profit for IT investment reasonable?

Resource:
- existing resourcing levels
- current Personnel policy with respect to recruiting new staff
- current Personnel policy with respect to temporary staff
- skill-mix within existing resource pool.

Whilst these may seem only too obvious, many IT managers will pay them insufficient regard in drawing up their grand plan. Along with those already mentioned – such as careful consideration of any relevant goals within the overall business plan – these simple factors should give the strategist a major steer in terms of where and how his proposals should be targeted. The objective must be to put forward a well thought out and appropriate strategy for acceptance by the business community. Indeed, I would be amazed if, after consideration of all the factors above, the manager would not be able – with a fair degree of certainty – to draw the boundary around his strategy thus: 'Two years; £1.9 million per annum; team of 16 people'. Doesn't that give us a head start?

Of course, another key contributor to framing the scale of the strategy will be consideration of the past. Within the current business, what has been tried but failed? What has been implemented successfully? There are many pieces to this particular jigsaw, and we would advocate not only getting them out of the box but also putting them picture-side up before attempting to complete the puzzle. There may well be a solid case for that multi-million, multi-resource, three-year project – but you need to be confident that it is appropriate and acceptable before suggesting it.

The last element of strategic 'scale' looks at the technical portfolio that might be proposed. Indeed, in consideration of what has or has not worked in the past, we have begun to touch on this. I believe it is important for the manager responsible for the strategy not only to have the tangible business parameters in his mind (time, budget, resource) but also general technical ones. These are broad-based, but can be answered with a few simple questions:

? Am I working in a completely 'green field' situation?

? Is there a well-defined – and hopefully proven! – technical environment, software and/or hardware, upon which the strategy must build?

? Is there anything that is a 'given', e.g. a global corporate directive?

? If numerous things having been of only limited success in the past, is there a need for some 'radical thinking'?

? Is there a need for general modernisation within the environment?

Being armed with this accumulated information – which should not be difficult to collect and collate – gives us the best possible chance of eventually producing a strategic plan whose ground rules and expectations are known and agreed.

At some point, you will need to define the person or persons responsible for driving the IT strategy forwards, and also address the issue of ownership. The unspoken default is, of course, that as we are talking about an IT strategy, the IT manager must be both driver and owner. Indeed, many senior business executives might well be fearful of having any responsibility for IT, particularly because (a) they do not understand it, and (b) many might only regard it as a 'necessary evil' in the first place. But as we have suggested, the IT strategy is part of the business strategy, and as such demands shared accountability. This is worth tackling here because the strategic plan should propose how the strategy itself is to be managed going forwards – if only to avoid the unspoken and inappropriate default occurring without appropriate debate.

The key question to be answered – and to this there should be an affirmative answer! – is 'does the business drive IT?' In the vast majority of cases, I suspect the response is 'not really'. Is the systems function a partner with the business in terms of IT initiatives, or is it re-active? And how is the business-IT relationship managed? I suggest that the strategic planner needs to be aware of this fundamental business-IT relationship because I am arguing for the strategic plan to contain a clear definition on ownership.

Of course, the answers may appear to vary according to company. At Big Bucks Inc., with its vast IT function, major policy is likely to be defined at the most senior of executive levels, with possibly numerous sub-strategies for the various parts of the business. The IT manager at Auto Partz is likely to report to the finance director, and at Gnomes 'r' Us, the person responsible for IT may we be someone in the finance function who doubles up on roles. Whichever of these scenarios, however, there is a fundamental relationship between the business community and the IT strategy, and as such the business must recognise this.

Whether it is called a steering committee, advisory panel, or IT board, a group needs to exist where the IT manager responsible for delivering against the strategic plan meets with those of his business peers who are looking to benefit from successful delivery. Such a group needs to be in place for a variety of reasons:

✔ to reinforce and maintain senior business commitment to the strategy

✔ to facilitate a communication feedback channel from IT to the business

✔ to enable the Business to keep IT abreast of developments which might invalidate elements of the strategy or change priorities. (Very often this is the most neglected of the three.)

Of course it would be possible to achieve this on a one-to-one basis with the IT manager meeting heads of departments individually, but we must not lose sight of the fact that the IT function is most likely a shared resource. What happens, for example, when both manufacturing and distribution initiate major changes that demand significant extra IT resource be devoted to their projects? The IT manager may not be able to satisfy both, and if he tries to do so not only will he fail both, he might also fail all his other business customers with a degradation of service everywhere. Under such circumstances, it is important that a forum exists at which the business can debate its use of IT and assign relative priorities, allowing the IT manager to act on their collective decisions.

Akin to this management issue is the related question of ownership. Who 'owns' the new warehousing system project; the warehouse manager or the IT manager? Again, the unspoken default is the IT manager. However, the answer to the ownership question comes from the response to the following: 'Who is to gain from the successful completion of the project?' If you are having a new garage built, who 'owns' the project; you or the builder? The builder may be responsible for the successful delivery of that to which he is contracted – but it is your garage, your money, and you who will gain the benefit. Why should IT projects in business be any different?

Business ownership of a project will primarily assist in the areas of commitment, feedback, and communication. And wouldn't it be useful if the steering group could be made up of those senior business people who 'owned' the IT initiatives ...

Of course, despite all the efforts of the IT manager, he may find it impossible to gain enough enthusiasm or commitment for any kind of business-IT link group. Worse still, he may not find a single peer in the business who is willing to sign-up to 'ownership' (and more on the subject of the sponsor later). Under these circumstances – the unspoken default situation – the manager will need his strategic plan (or Project Definition Report) to be as clear as possible in a number of ownership areas, many of which we touched on in Part One:

- his level and degree of authority
- how he will manage communication between IT and the business
- what actions he will take if he is unable to engineer the conditions necessary to deliver successfully against his obligation.

In such a situation, those assumptions and constraints we discussed earlier – and the management programme that accompanies them – takes on an even great degree of importance.

WHAT CAN HAPPEN...

The London Stock Exchange's paperless trading system, TAURUS

1987 - Taurus proposed at a cost of £60m; September 1988 - abandoned due to cost and opposition; 1989 - new version of Taurus proposed; February 1990 - estimated cost £40-50m; March 1990 - Taurus re-launched; May 1991/February 1992 - legal issues around Taurus; January 1993 - launch postponed to Spring 1994 (original target, October 1991); March 1993 - Taurus cancelled at a cost of £75m; July 1996 - Crest goes live in Taurus' stead, a 3-year development at a cost of just £29m.

The danger of needing to satisfy too many vested interests arose in the Taurus project where, as Flowers points out, 'it was not possible to propose a solution that ignored the interests of any significant part of that community.' It needed to be all things to all people, and was therefore doomed to failure.

The strategic plan basics

Thus far in this section of the book we have already considered a number of fundamental aspects relating to the definition of a quality

IT strategy: the importance of business goals and the business-IT partnership; the cultural and organisational terrain within which the strategy will need to operate; expectations and scale; and the issues of ownership and the management of the strategy. Given this as a backdrop, we are now in position to consider both the overall shape of the final proposal as well as delving a little further into the detail required for individual initiatives within the strategy.

There are innumerable different ways in which the final document could be planned, set-out and drafted, and these will vary according to preference, style and the demands of individual organisations. On this assumption, I will map out a possible structure for the finished article taking into account all we have discussed thus far, and walk through that. It may well feel that the final report would grow to be an over-large document and that your instinct is to cut back in certain areas; but please bear in mind that this should be the kind of document initiated rarely and its importance should not be underestimated. As with so much documentation produced from within an IT function, the quality of the Management Summary may be what counts.

I would suggest dividing the report into six sections as follows:

1. **Introduction**
2. **Management Summary**
3. **Positioning of the Strategic Plan**
4. **Individual Programmes and Projects**
5. **Summary**
6. **Appendices**

We will deal with each of these sections in a little detail, expanding the most on Section 4.

1. Introduction

Preface
A brief paragraph or two simply setting out the aims and intentions of the strategic plan, and possibly the document structure. Detail will follow elsewhere.

Document history
I suggest the insertion of a table to record version numbers,

modification dates, and the like. I will argue at the end of Part Six of this book that the strategy needs to be a living record, and therefore kept up-to-date throughout the period it is designed to cover.

2. Management summary

A précis of the major statements within the plan. Obviously this will need to be kept brief (no more than two pages) and as such may well lead to the predominance of bullet points rather than narrative. Things to definitely include will be: key assumptions; programmes or projects recommended; timescale, budget and resource assumptions; management plan; and next steps.

3. Positioning of the strategic plan

Background

A relatively brief statement covering the status of the current IT environment, positioning it on the Chaos-to-Simplification cycle. If relevant, this can also cover other aspects such as the status of individual systems, resourcing issues, and general IT considerations (such as e-commerce or the impact of the Euro). Also included here should be a view on the business-IT relationship and a broad statement on general business culture and ambition (as these relate to, or impact on, an IT strategy).

Business plan

Key drivers from the business plan to which IT can contribute should be highlighted here, including specific goals for each. There should be no business-related goal detailed in the next major section that is not first referred to here. Similarly, exclude any business goal that your programme is not designed to assist; this may help avoid confusion and/or false expectation.

Scale

Refer back to the Chaos-Simplicity statement to position the overall thrust of the strategic plan, i.e. remedial through to highly innovative. Also note any internal IT-specific issues here – such as the need to upgrade the local area network – as well as any other environmental influence, e.g. operating in a 'green field' site. We should also cover scale from the point of view of time, budget and resource here. This will frame the programme that follows.

Assumptions

Any assumptions relating to the general positioning of the strategy should be documented here. Specific project-related assumptions will be detailed in the next section. Hopefully there will be relatively few at this point, but remember to include assumptions relating to strategy management.

Constraints

As for assumptions, above.

*Note: by the end of this section your should have positioned your strategy in such a way that the reader is prepared for what is to follow. They will have an overall picture of your base assumptions, and a view of the business and technical environment within which you are working, as well as a boundary defined by the three key elements, **time, budget** and **resource**.*

4. Individual Programmes and Projects

Note: the initiatives contained in this section should be drafted according to a defined priority. If this is not achievable, ensure that there is some logical sequence driven by cost or delivery/implementation date. Remember that the strategic plan should cover the entirety of the IT function and therefore include not only programmes outside of business application development, but also maintenance programmes. We must ensure that the document represents a professional and comprehensive summary of the total plan for the IT function, and not simply a list of glossy, nice-to-have project ideas.

Project/Programme Name

Your initiative will need a title of some kind simply to enable people to talk about it succinctly! There is a traditional temptation to invent catchy acronyms for projects, but I would caution against doing this for any but the most important. Also avoid titles that are too obscure, clever or which may create a false impression. Sounds petty I know, but your users may get completely the wrong idea about projects called 'Flash' or 'Magic'!

Business Goal

State the business goal for which you are attempting to provide support. If possible quote directly from the Business Plan, or get the Business Owner to draft a sentence or two. Internal IT initiatives must also have a goal.

Measurable Business Target

Following on from the business goal, you need to identify associated specific and measurable targets. Like all objectives, these should be SMART – Specific, Measurable, Achievable, Realistic and Time-bound. This is an area where you may need input from the business. Additionally it would be useful to include here any parallel non-IT initiatives that are to be undertaken in an attempt to achieve the objectives set out. For internal IT projects – such as a network upgrade – measurable targets must also exist. Maintenance-type projects will also need to be made specific in terms of what is to be handled, e.g. calls per day; modifications per annum.

Business Owner

This should simply state the business manager responsible for delivering the business goal. Obviously there will have been significant contact between this person and the IT manager by the time the strategic plan is drafted (see the point above), and the business manager should be comfortable with the proposal – and supportive of it – before it is presented. Nothing looks worse that an initiative in a particular area which either surprises the executive concerned, or which fails to gain his or her support.

System Proposal

This is a narrative outlining the nature of the proposal. Obviously this can vary enormously in terms of length and detail, based on what is being suggested. An upgrade to an existing core business system might well be covered in a couple of sentences, whereas a major international package implementation would need to be considerably more expansive. Brevity and conciseness are the watch words here;

anything too verbose and you will lose your audience. For IT-specific proposals, you will need to ensure that the language used is particularly clear and free from technical jargon. Your business colleagues will be quite happy with 'orders', 'manufacturing output' and 'raw material stocks' but might just struggle with 'network bandwidth' or 'asynchronous processing throughput'!

Deliverables

All key concrete deliverables that have been identified to this point should be stated. You are unlikely to have planned the project in any great depth, but even if you have, stick to the big picture. Avoid detailed sub-deliverables at this stage – such as a Requirements Definition Document or Hardware Benchmark Report. The deliverables stated here should only be those that contribute to the business goal, and in many instances there may only be one per project. For maintenance-type programmes, there may not be an obvious deliverable, but if you have stated that the project is to 'improve internet access times by 25%', then you will need to recognise the deliverable(s) that allow you to achieve this.

Expected Business Gain

Having taken the trouble to analyse the 'now' of the existing business model, you will need to agree with the business owner the business improvement expected upon successful completion of this portion of the strategy. This is an important element of scale that can affect the project significantly. The difference between aiming at a reduction in month-end processing time of 10% versus 25% could be highly significant in terms of hardware investment for example. Also, making such a statement will remove the likelihood of any ambiguity and later disputes over systems performance.

Timescale

At this stage, you are unlikely to be able to offer much more than guidelines in terms of project timescale. Indeed, bearing in mind our horizon planning model, this is only to be expected. Rather than expressing specific end-dates, it would also be prudent to specify the timescale in terms of the elapsed period from the commencement of the project. If you estimate the project will take eight months, quote eight months; do not say 'November' in the expectation that the project will start at the beginning of March. When the project eventually kicks off in May, some people may well still expect delivery for November. (We will consider aspects of timescale planning later in this section.)

Resourcing

The situation with resources – including personnel, hardware, and software – is similar to that pertaining to timescale. State what you estimate you will need in broad terms, though if there are specific requirements or shortfalls that need to be addressed to be successful, say so. If having a database administrator is critical to the project – or new network servers, or an upgraded AS/400 – then be clear about it. The larger items will tie in with the budget, and will support any related assumptions or constraints you might choose to include. (Again, we will look at the resource planning a little later.)

Note: It is vital that any business resource needed on this project – for requirement definition, management, testing or whatever – is also explicitly included at this point.

Cost Summary

Quite simply, the cost of the initiative. Fundamentally this will include all resource costs, licence fees, training, expenses etc. Nothing should be omitted, and you should be as comfortable as possible that the deliverables set can be achieved in the timescale quoted with the budget suggested. As mentioned earlier, do not forget to include any relevant additional ongoing costs that you may incur as a result of the project, e.g. additional maintenance overheads.

Note: As the sum of all projects and programmes contained within the strategic plan should match the total budget requested or allocated, it is important that non-productive costs, e.g. holidays, administration, and sickness and general non-project related costs such a stationery, postage and photocopying, are included. This implies a section within your programmes and projects section to cover such items. Not very 'strategic', but important in terms of professional completeness.

Benefit Summary

Based on the expected business gains quoted earlier, some kind of quantification is required here. Usually this will be in terms of resource savings through efficiency gains, increases in business volume, reduction in waste etc. If, for example, you do speed up month-end processing in such a way that the annual work can be covered using 1200 work days effort in finance rather than the 1800 it takes now, then this 600 days saving is the benefit to be calculated – even though it may not be your responsibility to make the saving manifest (unless you have the authority to sack 3 people from the finance function, that is!). Whatever it may be, a summary of the financial benefits needs to be documented – and if the savings do not appear to be financial in nature, there should be a way to put a value to the business on them.

Payback Statement

Taking the cost and benefits statements above, provide a simple chart showing an estimated payback period. Annual numbers are usually sufficient, and usually no projections further than five years out would be required. The end of the period covered by the strategic plan may provide a suitable cut-off point.

Assumptions

As discussed in Part Two of this book and earlier in this section, detail any assumptions relevant to this project along with appropriate management actions.

Constraints

As for assumptions, above.

Risks

We will consider risk management in more detail a little later in the book, but for now it is sufficient to note that any risks specific to this programme or project must be noted here, again with appropriate management action.

Issues

As for risks, above.

*Note: There is often confusion between **risks** and **issues** – as there is between assumptions and constraints. I take a **risk** to be defined as a potential event that might compromise the successful execution of the project in accordance with the defined plan. This could mean a negative impact on time, resource, cost, quality or deliverable. An **issue** is an 'unknown' or an outstanding decision that may likewise impact the project. 'Poor performance of a software upgrade' is a risk; 'Awaiting a decision between deploying version 6.1 or 6.2' of the same package is an issue.*

Project/Programme Management

Having set out the initiative in this level of detail – and having identified owner of the business goal – you now need to propose how this particular part of the strategy is to be managed. You should nominate a business manager as sponsor of the project (more on sponsors in Part Four), as well as the mechanism best suited to overseeing progress: steering committee; advisory panel etc. You should also include a brief statement in terms of how you propose communicating feedback on progress. Remember, only promise what you know you can deliver.

Post-Implementation

Often omitted, some form of post-implementation process is necessary to close off the project. This is not only important to draw a line under the initiative and prevent the project from simply dragging endlessly on, it is also the time to revisit our proposed benefits and to see if they have materialised. This is usually the most difficult of tasks for two reasons. Firstly, if the IT project has been undertaken in parallel with some changes in business practice, it can be almost impossible to attribute benefits accurately. In these circumstances, simply note the overall gain. Secondly, there is often a reluctance on the part of senior managers – including those in IT – to actually recognise the benefits, i.e. make them 'real'. This is particularly the case where the aim has been to improve productivity and reduce staffing levels.

5. Summary

Project List
A simple list of each of the projects and programmes detailed above. If presented in tabular format, include key details such as bottom line costs and benefits.

Aggregate Figures
Aggregate all costs and benefits quoted into quarterly or annual estimates to show the overall IT spend and, hopefully, the overall business benefit!

Management Plan
Propose a management plan for the strategy itself. This will include overall ownership of the strategy and the corporate steering committee (or equivalent mechanism) which will drive it forward and ensure consistent relevance to and alignment with the business plan. As mentioned already, we will consider the updating of the strategic plan at the end of the book.

Next Steps
Based on when and how the strategic plan is presented, you will need to identify the necessary actions required to gain approval, budget etc. This will almost certainly vary from company to company, but it is important that a sign-off mechanism is agreed to ensure you have the authority to take the plan forwards.

6. Appendices

Any lengthy or complex calculations relating to figures or timescales quoted in the main body of the strategic plan should be included here. This is preferable to bogging down the main body of the report with pages of numbers, charts or graphs. All other supporting material should also be presented in the appendices.

Simple, isn't it!

At the end of the process, you should have built a comprehensive and well structured IT strategy aligned with the current business plan; your goals should be clear, and your deliverables evident. Hopefully the proposals will be coherently and well argued, in the main with suitable cost-benefit cases. Make no mistake, doing a quality job will take a little time, particularly in a complex environment or one where your responsibility is broad and range of business support extensive. It may, for very large operations, be appropriate to sub-divide the strategy into a number of plans based on business area, e.g. mortgages, pensions and investments in a large financial institution. In this case, a further complication of needing to cross-reference between strategies to ensure cohesion may add another element to be considered.

There is more to producing your strategic recommendations than somehow 'translating' the business plan however. You should never lose sight of the fact that, although you may be dealing with the plain text of a business plan, your key interactions will be with those business colleagues who you are trying to support. It might well be, for example, that the objectives set for the customer service function are phrased in a particular way, such that one course of action stands out above all others; however, in discussion with the customer services director, it soon becomes apparent that he has his own slant on the objective as stated in the business plan, and that he has a longer term view which has, as yet, to be committed to paper. This may put a completely different perspective not only on the business goal, but also on the options for its resolution.

Lientz and Rea also suggest that presenting multiple projects helps enlist a broad range of support across the business for any IT strategy.

Discussions with business partners may well reveal elements of these 'hidden agendas'. In playing the part of politician, the IT strategist needs to recognise not only what is important to the business, but also what is important to the business managers. If they have a particular vision or 'hot spot', then it is important that satisfaction of these is accommodated in the overall strategy if at all possible. The objective in doing so is to ensure support for the strategy. Obviously you would not want to compromise the integrity of the overall package –

supporting Lotus 1-2-3, for example, if a particular director was a devotee but the organisation was endeavouring to standardise on Microsoft Excel – but there is much to be said for prudent compromise and accommodation.

WHAT CAN HAPPEN...

'The Executive did not consider how all the projects related to each other, and overall the strategy lacked coherence.'

Committee of Public Accounts reporting on the 1992 and 1998 Information Management & Technology Strategies of the National Health Service Executive

---

One other group that needs to be borne in mind is the collection of individuals that make up the IT function itself. In discussing recruitment earlier, we said that it was important that you believe in the project for which you were attempting to recruit. Equally you must believe in the strategy you are putting forward. Not only that, the programme needs to be stimulating for your staff too. If they are presented with a strategy that suggests nothing but maintenance work for the next two years, then it is easy to foresee some of your best people moving on. On the other hand, if there are some opportunities to learn new things – exposure to new hardware, innovative technology and new package applications, all with the prospect of associated training – then it will be easier to keep staff motivated.

In considering this – along with those 'subterranean' motivations from senior business managers – the IT strategist needs to ensure that the final plan not only delivers business benefit, but that it also strikes the right kind of balance across all parts of the organisation. No mean feat this, but one which carries enormous benefits if successfully accomplished.

So, finally you have a document that represents perhaps weeks of work and which, you hope, will be widely applauded. You are sure that individual business executives will support the initiatives relevant to their areas, and – having run the whole thing by a couple of the senior members of your IT team – you are comfortable that it hangs together as a whole. This latter step is always a worthwhile exercise, by the way; often it will help to remove errors and jargon, and may enable you to hone one or two of your ideas. Never produce the strategy in a complete vacuum!

You feel ready to go public; but how? A suggestion as to approach.

1. **Run through the whole plan** with your immediate superior to ensure that you will gain their support for the strategy proposed. Be prepared to make some adjustments, but if you no not believe their suggestions are appropriate in any way, fight your corner.

2. Once you have a draft you are both happy with, **arrange a meeting** (at least a week hence) with the body whose buy-in you need. In the majority of instances this may well be the organisation's Board.

3. **Circulate the Management Summary** to each of the attendees of this meeting in advance. (Some may come back with suggestions and alterations, but resist these. Only make amendments with the blessing of your own manager.)

4. **Prepare a presentation** of the major highlights of the plan. This will obviously include a brief overview from the positioning portion of the plan, a summary of the main programmes and projects, and a conclusion including aggregate figures and proposal for ongoing management of the strategy.

5. **Prepare full copies** of the plan in a professional format for distribution on the day.

6. At the meeting, get your **manager to set the scene** and introduce you and the plan (gives immediate support). Make your presentation and take no more than 40 minutes. The questions which will inevitably follow may well lead the discussion to wander a little; but hopefully the chairman will be able to keep order!

7. At the conclusion of the discussion **gain clarity in terms of overall support** and what happens next. Never leave the room with the strategy 'hanging' and no clear indication of what happens next, i.e. you need to know how to get 'sign off'.

Once you have the 'green light', get down to work!

Peters argues that the project manager needs to sell – 'it forces clarity, focus, drive, faith.' Nowhere can this be more important than for the overall strategy.

Things not to forget

There are a number of things that should always be at the forefront of the IT manager's mind when putting together the strategic plan, though their relevance – and potential inclusion – will vary depending on circumstances. The first of these, however – the 'Quick Win' – should be very much part of your strategic thinking.

Unfortunately, strategists often scorn quick wins as little more than an irrelevant diversion; usually this is in the mistaken belief that a strategy needs somehow to be 'grand', and as such only worthy of lofty ambition. How then might we redefine the quick win? Perhaps those initiatives which are:

- low cost
- low risk
- giving immediate – if limited – benefit
- in application terms, often stand alone or as a rough prototype for something else
- occasionally remedial or stop-gap.

These do not sound like particularly meritorious attributes for projects to be included in a comprehensive IT strategy, do they? However, judicious use of the quick win can offer a number of significant plus points to an overall programme.

✓ They might be used to satisfy some of those hidden agenda items or 'hot spots' for a particular business manager. A useful, low risk/low cost way of gaining further support.

✓ They can provide opportunities for IT staff outside of mainstream work, perhaps as training opportunities.

✓ If used in a prototyping mode – perhaps to prove some element of Business Process Re-engineering – they might help prevent significant spend on projects that ultimately might be unable to deliver the benefits expected.

✓ They can also improve the overall Cost-Benefit equation in that they offer some benefits reasonably quickly. (If business executives are asked to commit to spending £3 million without a penny return for at least two years, how do you imagine they might feel? A little nervous perhaps?)

Again, inclusion of such small scale projects poses another question of balance for the IT manager; he would certainly not want to sacrifice the overall integrity of his programme for a few cheap thrills. So look for business goals which are themselves relatively small scale and seeking limited, but important returns. Seek out the projects which – usually PC-based – can be resourced by a single individual and completed within a month. Indeed, you may wish to set yourself a limit on such projects in terms of resource commitment: perhaps a one-person working month in terms of effort, and a limited budget for software or hardware.

As far as the strategic report is concerned, quick wins can be included in three ways:

1. as an element in a programme to tackle a single business goal, e.g. in 'proof of concept' mode

2. as projects in their own right, addressing individual business goals

3. grouped together in their own section, prioritised independently of the main body of the strategy – though one might counsel against this as it offers a ready made package just waiting to be cut from the budget!

Of course, whatever the mix of major and minor application development projects, or infrastructure, networking and communication initiatives, one area upon which the IT strategy can have an impact is that of organisational shape. We already hinted as much when referring to resource constraint – the need for a database administrator – during our overview of the basic structure of a strategic plan. Without doubt, the IT manager will need to keep the profile of his team in mind when drafting the strategy – both in terms of skill set and management hierarchy – but in doing so he should be careful to ensure that this does not overly compromise his ability to deliver benefit to the business.

Once the bones of the strategy are in place – i.e. you have settled on your major projects and programmes – it is prudent to step back and take a view as to the IT organisation needed to support it. You should have already begun to look at resourcing for each initiative, so will not be starting from scratch. A simple example will help to see why this is a prudent step at this point.

Perhaps you have a team with three project leaders with application development expertise. What happens if you are proposing a strategy that indicates that you will run four full-time projects concurrently? Immediately you might identify the need for a fourth project leader. Can you recruit? Is there someone on the lower rung of the ladder ready to step up? But what if you have identified only two major projects? What will you do with your 'spare' project leader? Is there another role this person can fulfil? If you can sit both current and ideal organisation structures side by side, then such mismatches should be immediately apparent.

And it is not only issues of seniority and experience which may surface. Perhaps you have a 60/40 split between development and operations staff, and the strategy calls for something akin to 70/30 – though with the same number of people. Perhaps the deep hierarchical structure that has been in place to-date (because the majority has been working on that one big project) now needs to be replaced by something much flatter and more flexible in order to enable delivery of multiple projects within the new strategy. Whatever the issue, it is unlikely that the organisation you have now will be exactly right for the strategy you propose, and you need to be clear about potential impact before you finalise your plan.

If it appears that you need to undertake significant reorganisation you may need to get the personnel department involved. If you need any radical changes, it will be essential that they have been accepted prior to your publishing your plan. Additionally, if some kind of restructure were required, then it would be prudent to include a summary of this in your strategic plan, probably in the final section. Having a clear resource plan to support the strategy will not only demonstrate thoroughness and help gain credibility, but it will also help development planning for the staff you have, and the definition of job specifications for the staff you will need to recruit. When considering your organisation, I would advise that you review your plans to manage succession. Take your organisation chart and one by one, imagine each box on the chart becoming empty. In your mind you should have another name to fill each and every vacated space; if not, think about it, particularly for key positions. Succession planning will help guide your career development planning too, and help staff motivation. This may not be something that needs inclusion in the strategic plan, but ultimately your ability to deliver against your commitments will be dependent on having the right people in the right places and at the right time.

Finally it would be prudent for us to consider the implications of drafting the strategy in a multi-site environment. Before brief consideration of how we might approach this, a word on the international dimension.

It is not inconceivable that in larger organisations your strategy might need to be set at a European, or even global, level. Whilst this does not invalidate any of the approaches suggested thus far, it does add a significant layer of complication. This comes about not only in that the 'hidden agendas' you need to address are multiplied many times – first nationally, then by business executive in each location – but also in that an approach which may be perfectly valid in the UK might, for example, be a non-starter in Italy on the basis of scale, business practice or even legality.

Before embarking on any kind of 'shuttle diplomacy' as you extend the net of your preparations overseas, you need to be clear in terms of your relationship with the your international affiliate. Very often they have their own IT departments with local reporting, and may not respond well to 'interference' from corporate headquarters. (Actually this is not uncommon amongst different UK locations within the same corporate organisation!) Key to any kind of productive and co-operative discussion must be the following:

- a clear and agreed relationship between yourself and the affiliate (i.e. between the group centre and its satellites)

- an understanding of the task with which you have been charged
- establishing a sense of mutual benefit from development of a strategy which all parties can support

The international aspect of any proposed major implementation might actually invalidate the approach to be taken in the UK as a corporate solution; this might lead to different deliverables on a territorial basis, all aimed at achieving the same goal. Defining a workable strategy is not simply a question of picking up the German or French business plans (if these are distinct entities) and applying these additional goals to the ones you have already been working with. It is a question of going through the process of understanding country by country: what is their culture? how do they operate? what is their systems environment? what are the local agendas? ... and so on. Such an undertaking makes production of the Strategic Plan a massive challenge and will consume a significant amount of time. Indeed, if you really are looking at a global strategy – and you want to do it right – then you might need six months! The message must be – as with your local business colleagues – try and ensure buy-in because support will be critical. And remember this can all apply to Bristol, Newcastle and Manchester as much as Belgium, Spain and Italy.

If one of your key strategic programmes is a multi-site roll-out of a single business solution, then ensure that you consider the implications of the following:

- phased or 'big bang' implementation
- technical environment at each location
- organisational structure to support the implementation – both locally and from the 'centre'
- increase in project time particularly for testing and training, though earlier stages may also be affected
- increase in budget to cover significant travelling and accommodation costs (almost always overlooked).

Lastly, if the roll-out is an international one, then in addition to the suggestions above you will need to add the complexity of language and time zones – for example, a 'big bang' implementation may well require work to be carried out in the wee hours! Under these circumstances you need to be wary of package implementations particularly. Some companies will attempt to sell you a multi-lingual, multi-currency package as a single solution; it is only later that you discover that the Italian version is developed and supported in Milan, the German version in Berlin, and so on. Under these circumstances you may actually end up implementing lots of different versions of the software – which can mean that any company specific modification you require will need to be made across all versions, and that there will be no such thing as a 'single' upgrade. The system may well 'save' three IT staff in the UK – part of the project justification – but if it means you need an extra two people in seven other locations for support ...

In proposing a single international solution to a single business objective, you will need to be particularly wary, especially when it comes to estimating timescales for implementation.

The numbers game – 1

One particular difficulty facing the IT manager as he drafts his strategic plan is the provision of estimates – time, resource, cost and benefit – which are robust enough to stand the test of time. This process is made especially difficult without diving to the level of detail that will eventually lie behind individual project plans once all tasks have been broken out, the critical path assessed, and resources allocated. By definition then, when working on numeric details for the strategic plan, the manager is largely working with generalisations, i.e. he is in that dangerous area known as the 'ballpark'!

Key to successful execution of this activity must be the overriding priority of needing to be realistic – though what does this mean exactly? The manager will certainly have a number of pointers at his disposal such as knowledge of his likely budget, and awareness of pressures from the business towards particular deadlines; but his greatest asset will be his experience and, ultimately, his 'gut feel'. Most managers will know whether Project A 'feels' like it will take two months rather than four, or that Project B must take at least a year and will need to be broken into some kind of phased delivery. Whilst it is not possible to teach this kind of instinct – nor describe how it works – we need to recognise the importance it plays; and hence, why it is valid to run your draft plan by other senior IT professionals to draw on their 'gut feel' too.

The variables the strategist has to work with are, as usual, time, resources and budget, though he also needs to be mindful of less tangible entities such as:

- **complexity** – of the solution and/or the political environment into which it will be delivered
- **experience** – both of the IT team and the user community with reference to developing and working with the tools that make up Project X
- **size** – how many modules are being implemented in the package (different to complexity), or how many new PCs are being rolled out across the country?

It would be useful if there were a magic formula into which you punched values for a number of variables and out popped the right answer. There isn't – and if someone tries to sell you one, don't buy it!

As if this weren't difficult enough, I strongly recommend that your estimates should be put together in such a way as to give you maximum confidence that you will not need more. Approach the budget in particular with the view that you can go but once to the well, and that when you eventually come to plan the work at project level (i.e. in detail) your ballpark estimates will be close enough. This is partly why I suggested that everything associated with a strategic initiative – including things like ongoing maintenance and impact on the disaster recovery plan – should be included up-front. And remember to include your calculations in an appendix so that you can justify every pound or dollar you have asked for.

For the purpose of the strategic plan, the spreadsheet offers probably the simplest and best method for presenting summary level numeric data (and any detail to be included in the appendix too). Keep the aggregated data as simple as possible, thus:

Budget	Period 1	2	3	4	5	6
Manpower	25	40	45	45	35	15
Hardware	125	35	10	10	25	5
Software	35	35	20	20	20	20
Expenses	5	10	10	15	15	10
Sundries	5	5	5	5	5	5
Total	195	125	90	95	100	55

In this simple example, the periods would be months, quarters or – as an extreme – half-years; the budget would normally be shown in thousands. Such a simple chart, when including benefit data, enables a quick overview of the financial aspects of the project to be gleaned. But how do you come up with the numbers in the first place?

I will now suggest a process that can take you from initial idea to an outline plan covering time, resource and budget. This method is applied on a project-by-project basis and, in doing so, it is important for us not to lose sight of the fact that we are working at the strategic level, and therefore any natural instinct we may have to delve too deeply into the detail will need to be curbed!

The first element in this process is definition of the **Key Stage Path**. In this worked example, I am making the assumption that our final goal is the implementation of a single business application across three different locations. There are some constraints that will be imposed on the project, but initially we operate as if this were not the case.

Key Stage Path

This is produced by defining all key concrete deliverables for the project from beginning to end. Once this has been carried out, a simple flow chart is drawn to represent how we would logically step through the various stages of the plan, with dependencies indicated.

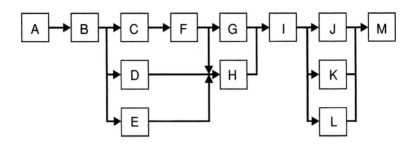

In our example, above, we have identified twelve key deliverables, e.g. 'A' is production of the Project Definition Report; 'I', a user-tested and signed-off system; 'J', 'K', and 'L' production systems in each location; and 'M', the Post-implementation Review. All concrete things and, as you can see, there are obvious dependencies – 'J', 'K', and 'L' are all dependent on 'I' etc. At this stage we have ignored any constraints upon the plan.

Key Stage Timeline

Our next step is to turn the Key Stage Plan into a Key Stage Timeline. This is achieved simply by making an assumption – based on your experience and that 'gut feel' we talked about – as to the length of time (elapsed) it would take to deliver each of the elements of the project. In our example, we believe that it will probably take a month to produce the project initiation document and get it signed-off. Similarly, we estimate that turning our user-tested application into a production system will take a month at each site.

Period															KEY STAGE TIMELINE
1	2	3	4	5	6	7	8	9	10	11	12	13	14	15	
A	B	C		F	G			I		J	M				
		D			H					K					
		E								L					

As you can see, the deliverables are now arranged back-to-back against a timeline that in this case represents fifteen months. The dependencies we noted in the Key Stage Plan are honoured through the relative positioning of the stages against our timeline.

Once this elapsed estimate has been made, in producing our First Cut Timeline we can start to consider the constraints we might need to address before successful delivery. For the project in question, for example, we have decided that it would be unwise to attempt the three implementations in parallel, and will therefore undertake them in sequence. When we now redraw the Key Stage Path to produce the First Cut Timeline, we do so taking such factors into account. Below is how our First Cut Timeline now appears:

Period							FIRST CUT TIMELINE							
1	2	3	4	5	6	7	8	9	10	11	12	13	14	15
A	B	C			F	G			I		J	K	L	M
		D		E		H								

As you can see, 'J', 'K', and 'L' are now arranged in sequence. Additionally we have decided that it would make sense to run 'D' and 'E' serially, but in parallel with 'C'; and that deliverables 'G' and 'H' really need to be produced at the same time (this lengthens both 'C' and 'H'). This is the stage to consider where there might be multi-threading opportunities, i.e. running potentially independent elements of the project in parallel even though our initial Key Stage Path may not have indicated such an approach. The effect of these practical adjustments has been to push out completion of the project from the end of period twelve well into period fifteen.

(Note: For this example I have assumed that we are approaching our Strategic Plan from a 'green field' position. I am also assuming that we have yet to develop our horizon planning model. If the latter were not true, then we might expect considerably more detail for periods one through three than shown, and possibly a little more from there until the end of period six.)

The First Cut Timeline now becomes the input into production of our next refinement that is where we begin to take human resources into account. It is sensible that this next stage in the process does not follow on immediately from production of our First Cut Timeline. A break is useful, with a review of the timeline a prerequisite before carrying on.

This review could usefully include tapping into the experience of other members of the IT team, as indicated earlier. The eventual impact of an error in logic or an absent key stage will be compounded from here on, so take the time to validate the work thus far.

In production of the Resource Timeline, we simply consider each deliverable and estimate how many full-time resources would be needed – IT 'internal' team; external IT resources, such as consultants; and user resources – to successfully achieve production of the deliverables within the timeline suggested.

RESOURCE TIMELINE

Period															
1	2	3	4	5	6	7	8	9	10	11	12	13	14	15	

A	B	C		F		G			I		J	K	L	M

	D		E			H	

I:	4	5	9	9	8	9	9	7	7	7	7	6	6	6	4	103
E:	1	1	4	4	2	2	3	3	3	3	3	2	2	1	1	35
U:	0	1	6	6	2	1	1	1	2	2	3	5	5	5	2	42

As you can see, the format chosen for the First Cut Timeline is easily adapted to allow annotation of our estimated resource needs ('I' is Internal IT; 'E' is external IT; 'U' is Resource from the Business). Thus, in period four, where we would be working on deliverables 'C' and 'E', we estimate needing a total of 19 resources in order to meet the deliverables according to the timeline, i.e. at some point early in period five.

Having produced a Resource Timeline we are happy with, we need to consider any resource constraints. In the case under examination we believe that we might face three:

1. that we are unlikely to have more than 8 internal IT staff working on the project
2. that it may be difficult to get more than 3 external consultants with the necessary experience
3. that we will be pushing our luck to try and get more than 5 business resources allocated to the project at any one time

In taking these constraints into account, it is obvious that we will need to adjust the elapsed time for some of our stages – the work has not reduced, so we need to expand the elapsed time to cater for the constraint on resource. In doing so, a Smoothed Resource Timeline would now show the project not ending until period sixteen. Unfortunately – and here comes another constraint – we believe that the business needs the system to be delivered and the project completed by the end of period fifteen. Consequently we need to undertake a different kind of adjustment, i.e. to seek out those periods where we are utilising less than our maximum allocation of resource to see if we can shorten any stages by increasing the resource working on it.

In our example you will see that we have slightly extended the elapsed forecast for tasks 'C', 'D', 'E', 'G' and 'H' – to take into account the over-commitment on resource – and that we have reduced the elapsed estimate for task 'I' by increasing the manpower assigned to it. The final version of our Smoothed Resource Timeline appears as follows:

Period															
SMOOTHED RESOURCE TIMELINE															
1	2	3	4	5	6	7	8	9	10	11	12	13	14	15	
A	B		C			F		G			I	J	K	L	M
			D		E				H						
I: 4	5	8	8	8	8	8	8	8	8	8	6	6	6	4	103
E: 1	1	3	3	3	3	3	3	3	3	3	2	2	1	1	35
U: 0	1	4	4	4	1	1	1	2	3	4	5	5	5	2	42

You will note that the estimates of total working months effort required – 103, 35, and 42 – are the same here as they were before we performed our resource smoothing exercise. This is an important check, as you need to ensure that you have not compromised yourself in terms of required effort.

Our Smoothed Resource Timeline now takes into account that target end-date as well as anticipated restrictions on resource numbers. Production of this part of the plan can be made easier using project management software such as Project Manager Workbench, Super Project Expert, or Microsoft Project; however, it is important that you keep the plan this simple and do not get seduced into detail or unnecessary intricacies.

Production of the Smoothed Resource Timeline again gives us an opportunity to undertake some quality assurance within our team to verify that the proposal still maintains the necessary degree of practicality. In the event of your having no steer from the business in respect of end-date or likely available resource, now may also be a good time to discuss your initial planning assumptions with your business sponsor. Check and verify before you move on; it can only improve the quality and viability of the end product.

The remaining step in this part of the strategic planning conundrum – 'remaining' yes, but paradoxically not the last! – is to put a cost against your proposal. This is achieved in two jumps, and delivery of the Budgeted Timeline is the final output.

The first of these two enhancements is the calculation of the cost of proposed resource ('R' in the chart below, with figures shown in thousands). As we already have proposed working months of effort, this first figure is arrived at by simply multiplying the figures shown by a working month rate. In our example we have used £5,000 per month for internal IT Resource, £10,000 for external, and £2,000 for business resource.

> *Note: Not all companies will require the inclusion of the monetary cost of business resources against the project. You need to agree the approach before you undertake this calculation and, in any event, state the basis on which the calculation was made. If your project requires dedicated, full-time user resource then I would advocate putting the cost in; this will allow your business sponsor the flexibility to back-fill for the people he allocates to your project – and if that cost comes from your project budget rather than his own, you will have found a friend!*

Having calculated resource costs, we can now do the same for hardware, software, expenses and sundries. Different projects may have slightly different cost breakdowns. For example, an e-commerce project where your company is offering its customers free access to your extranet may involve your footing the bill for the costs of associated telephone traffic charges. Again, the model we have been developing can be used to show this newly calculated data.

Period	**BUDGETED TIMELINE**														
1	2	3	4	5	6	7	8	9	10	11	12	13	14	15
A	B	C			F	G			I		J	K	L	M
	D		E			H								

	1	2	3	4	5	6	7	8	9	10	11	12	13	14	15	
R:	30	37	78	78	78	72	72	72	74	76	78	60	60	50	34	949
H:	25	25	10	5	0	0	0	10	0	0	10	15	15	10	0	125
S:	20	15	5	5	5	5	5	5	5	5	5	10	10	10	5	115
E:	2	2	4	4	4	4	4	4	4	4	4	6	6	5	2	56
O:	2	2	2	2	2	2	2	2	2	2	2	2	2	2	1	25
	78	80	99	94	89	82	82	92	84	86	99	93	93	77	42	1270

The Budgeted Timeline gives us a financial breakdown of the project by area – software, hardware etc. – as well as by period. We can also see the overall cost of the project; in this case estimated at £1.27 million. You would also like to add 10% contingency on this, making a total sum of £1.397 million. As with user resource costs, all costing assumptions need to be documented; this will be particularly useful in justifying significant expense budgets, especially those involving flights and accommodation. As I have said before, try and include everything you can think of. In our example here, post-implementation maintenance is being handled within the overall maintenance programme; if this were not the case, we would need another stage – 'N' – to cater for this (and 'N' might well stretch on for many months).

Of course, it is at this point that the final key constraint may bite. We have devised something which is fine in terms of both timescale and resource, but unfortunately we believe (or have been told) that the project will need to deliver in under £1.25 million to get the support needed. Logically this may seem something of a nonsense as we have yet to look into the benefits the business will gain from this project. Indeed, the £1.397 million we are suggesting could prove to be something of a bargain. However, in the real world such constraints do exist and need to be recognised.

Note: If you find you are unable to deliver what is needed within the timescale for less than £1.397 million, then argue your corner – but still be prepared to lose!

91

Realistically there is a reasonable chance that something in your plan will be unsatisfactory; and usually this will be associated with time, resource or budget. The process outlined above should be regarded as an iterative one, and if you need to find ways of delivering in less time, with less resource or for less money, then work back through the planning process, attempting to refine as you go along. If you are unable to satisfy all the constraints you face, then try repackaging the project. In our example, if the target for implementation at the main site had been set at period twelve, we might consider splitting the project into three; headquarters, then each of the other two sites. This would certainly allow us a better chance of meeting the first target date – though overall costs and timescales might well slip out as a result.

There remains one fundamental question which, depending on your approach, may well involve a review of the Budgeted Timelines you will have produced for your individual programmes: 'How do you show the timelines in your Strategic Plan; (a) as separate, independent schedules, or (b) linked into a single mapped proposal?'

The advantages of the former are obvious: complete a series of Budgeted Timelines – including those for maintenance and admin programmes – and you are home free. Or are you? Let's say you have outlined the following projects:

Project	Elapsed Months	Working Months	Budget
A	15	180	1,397,000
B	6	18	200,000
C	12	60	600,000
D	4	30	250,000

What happens if the business approves them all and, because of the way they are presented, expects all to start on 'day one' with the projects arriving in the 'D', 'B', 'C', 'A' sequence suggested, and all within fifteen months? The very real possibility will be that neither you nor the business will have the resource to handle four projects simultaneously, i.e. you will have come up against additional constraints, for example total resource availability. Some of the people you want on Project 'A' may need to be on Projects 'B' and 'D' too. And so on. Or perhaps running four projects concurrently – while viable from a resource viewpoint – may blow your annual budget.

Producing an overall plan, including all four projects spread over a longer timeframe – say 24 months – prepares a programme that would handle your getting the green light for all. But how should you go about this? You have two options.

- The first of these is to take each of the Budgeted Timelines you have produced – including, most importantly, the resourcing details that lie behind them – and schedule them together at their current level of detail. For this you would certainly need project management software, and it could well prove to be a very time-consuming task.

- Alternatively you could use the same process defined above – from Key Stage Plan onwards – to give you a first cut overall plan. How? Try simplifying each project to a reduced number of 'boxes', and then progress from the Key Stage Plan onwards. There may be dependencies between projects – a development project cannot be started until an infrastructure upgrade project has been completed, for example – but most likely you will have a number of parallel 'stages'. You already have resource and budget data from the more detailed work, so your concentration would then be on smoothing the resource demand as previously. This method is unlikely to provide you with as comprehensive a picture as the first approach – but it will give you a first cut much quicker.

One of the cons associated with producing an overall plan is that you will need to make a suggestion as to business project priorities; do you start with Project 'A' or Projects 'B' and 'D'? If presented individually, the business managers can decide – but remember they might just expect the impossible as suggested above!

My advice is to present each project as an individually planned initiative AND prepare a first cut overall plan using the simple method outlined to give an illustration as to how the separate projects might be married together.

The final set of figures required at this stage – and those which will ultimately give your whole programme credibility – are the estimates of benefit to be garnered from implementation of the various parts of the strategy. As we have already said, collecting appropriate benefit data is problematic for a number of reasons: it is fundamentally more difficult to calculate savings than spend; the user realm is often less adaptive to measurement than a project-oriented IT function; and there may be an innate reluctance for the business manager to go and 'collect' the benefit at the end of the project. These difficulties should not prevent the IT manager endeavouring to work with his business partners to achieve a reasonable result in this area. Indeed, some statement of benefit will need to be made otherwise where is the justification for the IT spend?

So, where can tangible benefits be found? Perhaps a number of areas such as: speeding up of existing processes; increase in business volume; decrease in business 'waste'; other efficiency gains (such as a reduction in errors); business process re-organisation; cost reduction. For each of the above, we will endeavour to give an example of how you might go about calculating benefit.

Example 1 – Speeding up existing processes

Currently it takes six days from an order being received in customer services (3 days) to the goods being shipped from the warehouse (another 3 days). Customer services have 3 people, the warehouse 7. 1,000 orders are processed each month. Assuming 20 work days in the month, the 1,000 orders therefore require 200 work days effort to be shipped (60 customer services; 140 warehouse).

Implementation of the new system will reduce the time taken for an order to go through customer services and the warehouse by a day in each, i.e. a reduction in overall elapsed time to four days. There is no backlog of orders and the number of orders will not rise as a direct result of this change. Therefore to process the 1,000 orders, the business now needs 40 work days effort in customer services and 93.3 work days in the warehouse. The implication is that after the change, those same 1,000 orders should be capable of being processed by 2 customer services staff and 4.7 warehouse staff. The saving could therefore be argued as the financial benefit to be gained by a reduction of around 3 staff.

The issue here will be in realising the benefit, i.e. making three workers redundant. The business may choose to 're-deploy' the staff concerned to other tasks, e.g. the ubiquitous 'improving customer service' or 'additional efficiency gains in the warehouse'. If they do, then you will need to try and define the benefits associated with this redistribution of labour.

Example 2 – Increase in business volume

The rail company currently has a four-band fare structure for standard class travel on its main routes. At present the computer system does not allow flexible seat allocation between these bands with the following effects: at certain times of the year and for various reasons – weekends, holidays etc. – each grade of ticket sells out quickly, but many remain unsold the remainder of the time. The result is that the company estimates only an average of 80% of tickets is sold per journey at an average price of £30. During any one year, these figures apply to 4,000,000 seats.

With the revised system allowing a flexible allocation of seats across bands to meet fluctuations in demand (within certain tolerances) the company estimates that it can pre-sell 95% of its seats, though with the average price falling to £27.50. Current income is set at £96 million. After the amendments to the system, this is expected to rise to £104.5 million – a net benefit of £8.5 million per annum.

This is the kind of benefit users will readily sign-up to. Firstly because it does not involve potentially difficult staffing issues, and secondly, if the benefits fail to materialise, they can blame the system!

Example 3 – Decrease in business 'waste'

In the present manufacturing environment, scrap rates are running at 4% largely due to inaccurate manufacturing forecasts from the logistics department. On a manufactured output volume calculated at £3,000,000, this equates to £120,000 waste per annum.

It is anticipated that implementation of a new forecasting system for logistics will halve scrap rates due to improved manufacturing forecasts. On this basis, the value of waste should reduce to £60,000 per annum. Additionally it is anticipated that manufacturing output will rise 10% year-on-year for the next five years, and therefore the scrap saving will increase proportionally. Again, another solid benefit which is open to clear measurement and verification.

Example 4 – Other efficiency gains

The existing web-based ordering system – which was effectively a pilot made 'live' – can only successfully process around 15,000 orders per day through restrictions in existing communications technology and networking software. It is estimated that around 5,000 orders per day may be lost as a result of customers failing to establish a connection with the ordering system, poor response times, and interrupted transactions. Each of these orders represent 20p profit to the company i.e. in a normal year, this equates to £365,000 lost profit per annum.

Upgrading the web system will increase resilience such that only 5% of orders should be lost, i.e. 1,000 out of the 20,000 currently placed (or attempted to be placed) per day. This represents a loss of profit of only £73,000 – an improvement of £292,000 per annum. It is anticipated that the volume of orders placed via the web will grow significantly, perhaps by 20% per annum.

Once again, a reasonably measurable benefit. When calculating the ongoing benefits – and taking that growth into account – these can be set against any increase in maintenance, support, licence fees etc. that the project will incur on an on-going basis.

Example 5 – Business Process Re-organisation

In an insurance company, the underwriting and claims departments currently utilise different business applications. Additionally they sit on different floors in the same building. Because of these factors, it takes the company a long time to process claims, and often the data passed between departments is less than accurate. Consequently, the company has a poor claims reputation in the market, and senior managers believe this is costing the business 10,000 policies per annum, each with a profit margin of around £25, i.e. a loss of profit of £250,000 per annum.

With the introduction of a new underwriting and claims system, the business intends to re-engineer its practices and set up combined underwriting-claims teams – split by regional responsibilities – with staff from the two disciplines actually sitting together. Senior managers believe that this will both improve the speed of claims handling and the accuracy of the data used, and therefore, raise the credibility of the function in the market. It is hoped that it will underwrite an additional 5,000 policies per annum as a result of this improved customer service, thereby generating an extra £125,000 profit per annum.

Although the number of policies can be accurately established, what is more difficult is measuring the positive impact of the new system as against the impact of the change in the business practice, i.e. setting up the new teams. The strategic plan should note the plans to reform business practice, recognise its likely positive impact, and quote the full benefit figure.

Example 6 – Cost Reduction

This area is often the easiest to identify because there is a direct saving to be had. For example, if something costs you £10 per item to order – combination of labour, system, postal etc. – and this is reduced to £9 per item, the saving is evident. Increasing the ability to bulk buy – because systems are providing more accurate forecast data – is another obvious example where unit costs fall.

There are many and various examples one could draw on here. Again, this is the kind of area which the business will readily support as the gain immediately benefits the bottom line and normally is void of people issues.

So much for our examples. But failing this kind of analysis, one tack adopted is to describe the initiative as 'strategic' to the business. This appellation is often applied to very large projects where calculations of benefits would take an age in themselves; often international implementations of corporate or group initiatives (particularly in the applications area) will be endorsed in this way. Saying a project is 'strategic to the business' may be another way of saying, 'Look, everyone knows we need to do this and that it's important for the long-term. We know it's expensive and that we can't quantify the benefits, but it's something we've simply got to do'. This is fine if the business accepts that proposition – and if it is indeed given as an argument for undertaking a project, then provide a little narrative akin to the above in the benefits section; don't say nothing – and don't quote figures you can't substantiate.

Whatever you do quote as the benefits to be gained from a particular project, ensure that the business owner agrees that those benefits are achievable before you go into print. When it comes to the debate, you need will to be supported by them.

Other considerations

Finally in this section on defining strategy, I would like to consider a number of subjects which, whilst not likely to be core elements of the final plan will, depending on their adoption, carry significant implications. These impacts could be in areas of budget, timescales, deliverables, or method of implementation, and yet can still be ignored when drawing up the plan. So, to prototyping, interfacing between systems, e-commerce and the internet, outsourcing, and personal computers. I make no attempt to give a comprehensive overview of each – subjects for another time, perhaps – but rather attempt to raise awareness of the issues involved.

Prototyping

A generally misused conception, most often prototyping happens almost by accident – and often leads to the 'productionisation' of an incomplete and inadequately tested system (application software or systems infrastructure). A prototype is an 'original model' (Collins English Dictionary); something which serves as an indicative precursor to the final deliverable. Most often, prototypes are used to model the application's interface between the system and its users, i.e. typically the 'look and feel'. Because of this, they are often built with limited functionality to simulate processing in a live environment. Modern development tools lends themselves to this approach because simple applications can be thrown together at short notice, and while they lack any substantive quality, they can actually look quite good. So good in fact, that before you know where you are, your user is already punching in real business data and the prototype has become business critical!

Prototyping obviously offers the most value in the development of bespoke business application systems. In addition to confirming 'look and feel', the prototype is also useful as a means of cross-checking the

IT function's understanding of the business process the system is being designed to support. Prototypes are less useful in small, standalone applications, and it is in this area they are most likely to become rogue production systems – and should therefore be most stringently avoided! A few suggestions:

✓ If a project in your strategic plan would warrant development of a prototype (through size, importance to the business, newness of the technological approach etc.) then remember to include the prototype as a deliverable and a Key Stage element.

✓ Be specific about the function of the prototype, i.e. 'to verify inter-screen navigation'.

✓ Be specific about the life span of the prototype – and remove users' access to it at the end of this period!

✓ If there is any danger – or historical precedent – that the prototype will become a production system, then you might want to seriously consider not prototyping at all!

Interfacing

Passing relevant data between associated but disparate business systems probably began to be a major problem in the 1980s. Prior to the growth of both PC technology and the package software market, the vast majority of businesses ran bespoke software running on large machines; systems which were tailored and expanded to create additional function, rather than having new function provided through a completely different application architecture. Over time, the prevalence of interfacing – and thus issues it brings with it – has grown, particularly as businesses migrate from one platform to another, from one chunk of software to another, or from a legacy environment to something more current. The need to interface between systems has also grown as individual business functions have been addressed by specific software offerings; Package X for finance, Package Y for manufacturing, Package Z for distribution and customer service.

The recent growth in Enterprise Resource Planning systems – such as SAP, Baan, Peoplesoft – is in part recognition of this trend; an attempt to provide a single, integrated suite of systems where the need for external interfaces is greatly reduced. Having said as much, I believe the interface issue is here to stay and, as such, bound to impact on at least one of the programmes outlined in any strategic plan which covers business applications. With this in mind, it is important to consider this element – and associated deliverables and key stages – when putting the plan together. Issues such as:

- impact on time, resource – and therefore cost
- the dependence on others: another project team; an external software vendor etc.
- additional layers of complexity over testing, i.e. you might have two systems to test now, if the interface is two-way.

One possible approach – and this could be an independent element of the strategy in its own right – is to develop a 'constant interface system', i.e. an application which acts as the gateway between any and all systems within the overall business environment. Built to the same principles as electronic messaging systems, such a 'data gateway' would provide a set of consistent data interface formats against which all communicating systems would need to comply, the idea being that once system 'A' had met these requirements, it could be sure that in taking its data, system 'B' would be able to deal with it. Also any data it takes in from an 'external' system would be of appropriate quality and meet specific criteria. Such an approach lends itself perhaps to a data warehousing environment too.

For the vast majority, the constant interface principle may well be overkill. But whatever the interface challenge you face:

1. make no assumptions
2. define an approach over which you have control
3. use what's already there and working.

E-commerce and the internet
Many people would argue that anything related to the internet or 'doing business electronically' merits individual attention or a special approach. I have to say that I disagree. From a management perspective, the issues faced in this area are exactly the same as those we have already discussed: timescale, resources, scope, expectation, budget, prototyping etc. Indeed, many people think that e-commerce

is a new phenomenon when in fact a significant number of large organisations have been trading electronically – passing orders and invoices – since the 1980s.

The internet has, of course, provided a larger (global!) infrastructure through which we can all now trade 'electronically', and with this quantum leap, the term 'e-commerce' has come into being. It is the term and the medium that is new, not the philosophy that lies behind it.

From the point of view of the strategic plan, that there must now be an internet element within it is a sine qua non. Do not forget it – but do not pretend that it is rocket science either. The business rules that apply to any 'standard' transaction will need to apply as rigidly as ever, but with key additional implications in areas such as security and communications. Indeed, for the first time, IT managers are faced with a situation where the success of a business application is actually more dependent on the technical environment that supports it than the application itself. Remember this when proposing an e-commerce business application, and start with the premise that your existing technical infrastructure will be inadequate.

Outsourcing

One part of the strategic plan that may relate more to management than anything else is associated with outsourcing. In that the most common element in this area is disaster recovery, it would be reasonable to suggest that probably 95% of strategic plans should carry some element of outsourcing within them. The motivations behind outsourcing are many, but normally stem from a 'lack' within the parent organisation – usually in terms of resource, expertise or availability of facilities. Disaster recovery is a good example therefore. Often, however, outsourcing is proposed in terms of a cost saving – a known product for a known cost.

From the perspective of this book, a few observations and questions in relation to outsourcing are in order.

? Are you planning to outsource critical elements of your strategy – and if so, should you really?

? Have you defined and agreed a management process between yourselves and the supplier?

? Are there clear and agreed deliverables in terms of the service you are to receive – and clear and agreed penalties for the supplier not meeting those commitments?

? What say, if any, do you have on the resources working for you?

? Are they a partner rather than a supplier?

? What is *their* agenda?!

? Could you do it cheaper?

This last question is always a good one to finish up with!

They key to successful outsourcing is the maintenance of control. All the things we have talked about thus far relate to the provision of a quality systems environment, irrespective of who is actually carrying out the work. Therefore, if you are committed to a quality programme, risk management strategy or whatever, then it is reasonable for you to expect – or insist on – your supplier doing the same thing. If they are providing a key service – say an extranet service to your most valuable customers – do they buy in, not only to your strategy, but also to your way of managing the strategy? For me, outsourcing equals relinquishing of control; so if you do pursue any kind of outsourcing programme, ensure you are confident you have the control you need.

Personal Computers (PCs)

It is virtually impossible to get away from the PC in a modern business environment. Its power and flexibility is becoming more and more critical to functions such as finance, sales, and customer service; yet as more and more are deployed, the issues relating to such a move are often ignored. Any strategic plan in which PCs play a part – either as a stand-alone tool or as the vehicle for accessing core business systems – must address two key issues.

1. Does the PC 'belong' to the organisation or the user? Of course, the organisation – what else?! However, most users think of the machine as their own and resent any attempt to exercise centralised control over it; why shouldn't they have their favourite wallpaper or snowboarding game loaded ...? This is a thorny issue; be clear and firm, or die. Define a PC policy, get it

endorsed, then implement without exception. You may not be liked, but you'll have a better chance of keeping control.

2. Have you identified the full cost of the PC? Not £999 for the basic model, but also the software licence costs, associated printers, network traffic costs, upgrade/replacement costs, support overheads (in terms of 1 person for each 50 machines, perhaps? – more for laptops), some kind of help desk support infrastructure, replacement machines for 'hot swaps', virus control, control of internet access, hardware maintenance contracts, data backup and recovery etc. Basically, think of a number and treble it.

At the end of the day, PCs represent a major support overhead and an element of the systems environment that is difficult to control. It is unlikely that the IT manager will have much choice in the matter if his environment has PCs installed already, but minimising the cost of desktop ownership must be an objective and the strategic plan can be a good vehicle in helping to tackle this. Face the facts of PC ownership and perhaps ask:

- 'Do users really need PCs?'
- 'Would a net-station provide the functionality required?'
- 'If I went thin client, just how thin could I go?'
- 'Who really needs a laptop?'

And next ...

Hopefully in this section of the book we have provided an insight into the key aspects of setting out a strategic plan. We now move on to consider how to take an element of that plan and deliver against our commitments.

Part Four looks at the next logical step in the process, project planning; Part Five will take that on, and consider how we manage the subsequent project.

4

Project Planning Foundations

In our ordered and harmonious world, the IT manager arrives at the gates of his new project, the planning element immediately ahead, knowing that the work he is about to undertake forms an element of his recently adopted strategic plan. More than this, he goes into the project proper with a solid guide for the work in terms of time, resource and budget.

As we know, however, the world is neither particularly well ordered nor harmonious, and projects can be forced on the most thorough and diligent of managers at the drop of a hat. What follows in this part of the book is an overview of the project planning process: the foundations upon which a plan should be based; how the project itself should be organised; a review of how to arrive at the detail within the plan; and those additional factors that need to be considered before the Project Manager 'goes public'. This process should be valid whether or not the project has flowered from the germination of the strategic plan, or has arrived out of the blue, unexpected and – probably – unwanted.

In advance of putting a project plan together, it is important that the Project Manager addresses some fundamental philosophical and management issues in order to locate the plan within an appropriate business context. As with the strategic plan, expectations, ground rules, and ownership need to be tackled up front.

What is a project plan?

A simple enough question – but ask ten IT professionals and you are sure to get ten different answers. Ask ten business people and you may well get just one answer: 'It's one of those things that IT people produce with all those complicated lines and bars. It's nothing to do with me; I don't even understand it!'

Recognise that kind of response? IT people do, by and large, produce implementation plans, and often they are daunting and complicated – but if the business cannot understand the plan, it has failed. Also, the plan is **very much** to do with users; as we have already argued, an IT project is a business project and therefore it is critical that the business does not distance itself from the plan.

So, 'What is a project plan?' Perhaps most significantly, it is:

- a structured route map setting out what needs to be done in order to achieve a business goal
- a definition of the time and resources – IT and business – needed to complete the defined work
- a mechanism for tracking and managing the project to best ensure delivery within the allotted timeframe and budget
- a means of communicating progress.

Before committing anything to paper – and, more importantly, before pestering business colleagues for user resource to work on the project – it is critical that senior business partners both understand and accept the role the plan is to play in the project.

Assuming the Project Manager has managed a modicum of consensus on the above, he needs then to turn to the 'what' and 'how' of the project plan. Firstly this involves having a clear picture of the process he intends to follow in order to derive a workable plan, the structure of that plan, and how it will be drafted (e.g. use of tools). Secondly, it requires a statement as to how the plan will be managed; not the tasks represented on the plan, but the plan itself, i.e. the rules for plan management.

We will deal with the detailed planning process in a short while, but before we do so we will need extra preparation if the project has arrived on the Project Manager's desk out of the blue. Any scheduled project – based on the strategic plan – has already been subject to some background planning through the process that took us from Key Stage Planning to Smoothed Resource and Budget Timelines. The unexpected project will have none of this background, and, if it possesses some degree of significance in terms of business criticality, duration, expense etc., then the Project Manager should back-fill his planning by undertaking the high-level estimating process outlined for elements already in the strategic plan itself. Of course it is entirely likely that this new project will come with significant in-built constraints – a required end-date being the most likely – and in attempting to achieve the new goals now being set, the Project Manager will need to ensure that the impact on other, existing projects is not forgotten.

The issue of prioritisation is key here. Assuming that all IT resources are fully committed – and business resources too – then the new project will have a negative impact on existing plans, and the Project Manager needs to ensure that any revised priority is agreed by the business owners of his various projects and that the knock-on effect of the new work is understood. Failure to do so will lead everyone in the business to expect their particular project(s) to be delivered as scheduled – including the new one – without any changes whatsoever!

Needing to tackle such changes to project plans is another justification for stating up-front how any plan (or group of plans) is to be managed. The Project Manager will need a process and/or set of rules for the following:

- regular updating of the plan – daily, weekly, monthly – with identification of the data that will normally be modified at this point – typically actual hours/days worked and progress against or completion of tasks
- changes to end-dates for key deliverables
- lack of resource availability – particularly from the user community
- addition of major tasks and/or deliverables which impact the overall plan in terms of time, resource or budget (including, where appropriate, an escalation procedure for significant changes)
- deletion of major tasks and/or deliverables in an effort to 'de-scope' the project with a view to attaining timescale and budget targets (including, where appropriate, an escalation procedure for significant changes) – remember that deliverables should not be 'lost'
- publication and communication of the plan.

As we have already indicated, establishing the relationship between the project plan and the business is critical – and something which is often overlooked. Breaking through any ingrained status quo – i.e. of the business not recognising that the plan is relevant to them – is vital if associated issues of ownership and sponsorship are to be settled in favour of the project.

Given what we have said already, the answer to the question 'who owns the plan?' is most likely to be greeted with a resounding chorus of 'the IT guys!' It may be that the systems professionals put the plan together and manage the process for keeping the plan up-to-date, but this is a very different thing from ownership; and as we have already said, an IT plan is a business plan. To be most effective the plan should be owned by a senior member of the business community; preferably one with (a) a vested interest in the project being successful, and (b) the authority to allocate business resource.

Ownership, in this context means taking responsibility for the plan and any changes that are made in terms of dates and scope. For a business user this implies an understanding of the plan and a partnership with the IT Project Manager. By definition, this must imply a close working relationship between the two senior partners – business and IT – and a joint commitment to the success of the project.

Unfortunately, management of the plan – the Project Manager's remit – is almost without exception translated by the business into ownership, and thus the distancing begins. Worse than this, it is ownership without authority, and nowhere is this more keenly felt than in the Project Manager's attempt to allocate non-IT resource to the project. Under such circumstances – and assuming the Project Manager has failed in getting a business owner for the plan – the only recourse open to the IT manager is clear, consistent and regular communication.

Of course, the overall arbiter – and the individual who is most likely to nominate any business plan owner – is the project sponsor. If we are following through our logic from the strategic plan, the sponsor is most likely to be that business individual who provided the key support for the project during its embryonic stage, i.e. the business owner of the strategic business initiative.

Most often, a project sponsor is defined as that person who has the most to gain from the success of the project. The sponsor is supposed to be an individual with the authority to make things happen, and the general wherewithal to steer the ship. However, rather than being the Admiral (to the IT manager's Captain), most often the project sponsor is no more than a figurehead. Undoubtedly this is partly because they do not understand their role – and partly because they do not embrace it.

For project sponsors to be successful, they should:

- take ownership of the project plan – either directly or through the appointment of a senior manager with delegated authority
- sign-off on the benefits expected from a successful project
- sign-off on the initial project plan and any project definition report
- sign-off on key deliverables and at 'Go/No Go' checkpoints
- attend regular project progress meetings
- act as arbiter and ultimate decision-maker on all project matters when requested
- be visible, supportive and committed!

More often than not project sponsors:

- allow their name to be used without understanding the responsibility that goes with the role
- do not attend project meetings
- provide no feedback on reports sent to them
- abdicate/delegate all project decisions to junior staff (often without the authority to achieve anything meaningful)
- dish out the blame when the project fails!

A project's chances of being successful will be enormously enhanced with a knowledgeable and committed project sponsor. Without one, it becomes increasingly important that the Project Manager is explicit in terms of how he will manage the project and exercise his responsibility, and any project definition document may – as we have already said – provide the one and only opportunity for him to be clear on this.

'The danger of any IS project is that it becomes too technology focussed and ignores the wider organisational and political issues that surrounds the development.'

Stephen Flowers on the Taurus project

Organising the project

Once you have your project planning hat on, it will soon become evident as to the resource you will need to successfully execute the programme. From an IT perspective, this will most usually crystallise into a certain number of application development staff, a certain number of operations staff, and a degree of business user involvement. Obviously the profile will vary dramatically depending on the project – bespoke application development to network infrastructure upgrade – but the work carried out thus far, on Key Stages and the Resource Timeline, will provide valuable input. Indeed, based on the information gathered to-date, it would be prudent to attempt to draw up an 'ideal' project organisation before going any further.

The structure arrived at should answer questions such as:

? How many project leaders do I need?

? Do I have dedicated development resource reporting to them, or do they share a common pool?

? Would a mixed IT and business team be best for certain parts of the project?

? Does this project in itself – or in conjunction with other initiatives – lend itself to the adoption of a Project Office to handle all administrative matters?

In an ideal world, the Project Manager would have the resources available – with the necessary skills – to fill out this 'ideal' project organisation hierarchy, and he could then embark upon the detailed planning work in possession of one of those rare things, 'a warm, fuzzy feeling'.

In reality, the necessary resources are unlikely to be available either in the required quantity or with the required skill-set and therefore you might imagine that all the Project Manager would achieve by undertaking this exercise is to identify the gaps. This is only partly true; yet even so, this 'resource gap analysis' is a benefit in itself as it provides both the argument and the detail to support any recruitment or secondment initiative should this be available. What it also provides is a view of his major resourcing issues before the Project Manager starts planning.

Let us assume that we had identified two key stages that appear to be able to run in parallel. However, to achieve this, both require a dedicated database administrator – and the Project Manager has only one at his disposal. If recruitment is not an option, he is immediately aware of one of the significant choices he has to face when he starts to plan; does he run the stages sequentially, or keep them in parallel but double their elapsed time? Such dilemmas can offer opportunities too. Perhaps he has an individual who, with the appropriate training, could adequately function as the database administrator for one of these two stages. Recognising this – and therefore enabling the scheduling of training early on in the project – may address the shortfall. Obviously it is better to be aware of such things as soon as possible, rather than after you have spent two weeks putting together the perfect – but perfectly unachievable – plan.

We have already said how important it is for a project sponsor to understand his or her role in the project, and this is equally true for all members of the project organisation. In the example above, a newly trained database administrator is likely to have slightly less responsible tasks, and the senior one given a mentoring role. It is useful, therefore, for the Project Manager to provide a brief overview of the roles and responsibilities for all working on the project, from the sponsor down.

It is easy to get carried away at this point and produce reams of paper attempting to detail each and every facet of each and every role. Plainly this is a waste of time, but people do need to know what is expected of both themselves and those they are working with. On this basis I would suggest a simple pro-forma to cover:

- ✓ **Job Title or Role** – e.g. project sponsor; Project Manager; database administrator; user specialist
- ✓ **Duration of assignment and effort expected** – e.g. 6 weeks @ 2 days per week; full-time for 3 months

✓ **Main Function** (in a single sentence, if possible) – i.e. what they will be doing

✓ **Expected deliverables** – this one is key because it defines the concrete contribution to be made. Again, reams of detail are not required, simply enough to be specific – ideally with dates. For example:

- **project sponsor:** chair weekly progress meeting; sign-off key project deliverables
- **Project Manager:** produce weekly progress report; maintain project plan
- **user specialist:** define business requirements; acceptance test system.

Such a summary should cover no more than a page of A4 – and the deliverables should be such that, if they are not met, the project will suffer, i.e. they are important. Draft all the definitions, get them agreed with the sponsor, then circulate to all members of the team. Invite feedback; if people do not think they will be able to meet the commitment you expect – in terms of both time and deliverable – then you need to know now! By the way, such an exercise is also useful in helping identify the right people to fill any gaps.

At this stage, it is also prudent to outline any review processes or quality measures which you intend to apply to the project, though how much there is will depend on the type and size of the project. As before, the key is not to go overboard, but to be clear, concise, and again, to circulate the information in advance to all members of the team, users included. The summary should outline any (or all!) of the following:

- **Project Audit:** when will this be undertaken and who will do it – and have you included them on the team? They have a contribution to make!
- **Inspections:** what will be inspected – business requirements? programme specifications? – and who will carry these out?
- **Walkthroughs:** the same as above.

I exclude risk and issue management from this list as these form part of the Project Manager's role – and have hopefully been included in their role and responsibility summary! As with the work already carried out at this stage on the organisation, this element can assist in ensuring that an appropriately structured – and appropriately staffed – project team is put together.

The numbers game - 2

Many people regard the ability to put together a detailed and **workable** project plan as something of a black art. Indeed, there is much that goes into such an endeavour over and above any kind of formulaic process – or simply entering data into project management software and hitting some kind of auto-scheduling button! Experience – often of the painful variety – combined with wisdom and good old 'gut feel' help the Project Manager to undertake that most nebulous of tasks, attempting to make known the unknown, i.e. predicting the future.

Given that it is usually pretty difficult to forecast anything three days ahead – the weather being the notorious British example! – attempting to define what will happen on a specific project several weeks hence is pretty much akin to climbing Everest with one leg tied to a very large rock. Of course some misguided people think they can do it – remember the 11th of November Man? – but these poor souls are soon chastened by their experiences; unless they are particularly thick-skinned, that is!

Having said all this, project planning is not an activity that can be side-stepped because of its inherent impossibility. Perhaps the fundamental rule is 'Always be realistic'; you can bet your boots that if you think a task will take four days, but squeeze it to two in order to fit your plan, then the task will take at least four days and you'll end up kicking yourself mightily – as well as potentially wasting a great deal of management time.

If the planner approaches the beginning of the project and its associated planning task via the strategic plan and through the route already suggested, then he will already have some useful background material. Indeed, the first task should be to review everything from the Key Stage plan through to the Resource and Budget Timelines to (a) refresh his memory and bring him up-to-speed, and (b) to give the overall project something of a sanity check. Again, the need to remain realistic is paramount.

The second thing it would be useful to do is to set in context the plan he is about to produce not only within the portfolio of work carried out to-date and any other associated or related projects, but also in terms of any horizon planning model he might be following. If, for example, he follows a standard three month horizon for planning purposes, this will draw the boundary for the planning work he is about to undertake; it sounds trite, but do not plan a project in more detail of than you really need. Be aware of the next planing segment over the horizon, and add a little more detail only if it is appropriate or useful to do so – but do not follow in the footsteps of our 11th of November Man!

We considered issues relating to budget setting when defining the overall strategic plan. Many of these will equally apply to an individual project – particularly when there is no defined budget for the work to be undertaken (as with the 'unexpected' project). The task of arriving at a project budget should be approached with the principles of 'everything you can think of' and 'once-to-the-well' already discussed.

It is possible that the project budget may be a given, with the financial parameter either drawn from the strategic plan or imposed by some other mechanism, often arbitrary. Under these circumstances, the Project Manager may face a difficult decision when, on completing the detailed project plan, he finds the sum allocated to be insufficient. An iterative process will demand a revisiting of the plan of course, but often the Project Manager is forced to undertake cost-saving measures. With people likely to be the most significant element of the proposed spend, one reaction is to cut the number of days to reduce cost – even though such an approach could seriously compromise the integrity of the plan. There are a number of potentially more palatable options, each requiring varying degrees of sleight of hand:

- change the balance between expensive external resource and in-house resource
- consider explicitly removing the cost of any business resource

- see what resource costs (human and material) might legitimately be capitalised; though this does not reduce cost, it spreads it out, which may be acceptable (though beware the knock-on effect in later years)
- check for over-estimation in non-people areas, such as hardware, software, expenses etc.

Of course the actions suggested above should be undertaken with a great deal of care, the implicit truth being that any cut in an 'ideal' budget must increase the risk to the project in some shape or form.

Following the 'Horizon Planning' approach – and being given the authority to handle a project budget in the same way – gives the Project Manager the opportunity of firm assessment of the period immediately ahead, plus a gradual definition of that further down the road. The end result may be a project that is more expensive than the original ballpark estimates (and possibly later than imagined), but it may put you in the best position possible to deliver a well controlled, quality product. This method of 'increasing accuracy' – both in terms of timescale and budget – demands the acceptance of the fluid state within which horizon planning operates.

In addition, it also offers the benefit – if adopted across the entire IT environment – of a 'Rolling Budget' model. Rather than stab at any forecast spend perhaps eighteen months hence (which is what is normally required from standard budget cycles), the IT manager is able to give a regular update of his financial profile. Every three months, say, a revised budget is produced showing a firm budget for the next quarter with estimates of increasing 'softness' for the five quarters after that. If a streamlined process for producing these budget estimates can be arrived at, the trauma of the annual budget should be significantly diminished. Indeed, this could be a useful approach to adopt informally, even if financial estimates are required but once a year.

'The number of project failures could be dramatically reduced by making use of a 'step by step' progression of relatively small projects ... The advantage of such a structured approach is that it helps to reduce the complexity of planning, monitoring and control.'
Committee of Public Accounts

Defining a detailed approach to project planning is obviously something of a massive task; indeed numerous books have been written on this very subject. Given the scope of this present endeavour, I do not propose to attempt to undertake any kind of radical condensation of an entire theoretical process within these pages. What is appropriate, however, are some suggestions in terms of estimating cost, timescales and benefits in accordance with that which has gone before and the thoughts on practical project management and execution, which are to follow.

Estimating Cost

From a simplistic point of view, a project has only one cost: resources. These resources can be split into three component parts: human resources (people); physical resources (hardware, software, 'things'); financial resources (money itself). From a project perspective therefore, we can demystify the budgetary process by endeavouring to simplify it. Of course in doing so we may be consciously sacrificing pin-point accuracy; but remember, the 11th of November Man probably attacked his budget in the same way as his plan – and therefore with the same inevitable degree of inaccuracy.

Once you have a plan complete with tasks and work days estimates, calculating the cost of human resources should be achievable by multiplication. Once you have identified the hardware and software required for the project, again reaching a budget figure should be a question of simple mathematics. Not surprisingly, once you know where all the other project pounds are going – expenses, training etc. – again, rudimentary maths will be all that is needed.

So why do Project Managers find forecasting project costs so difficult? The answer is simple. Because they don't include everything they should do. We might also ask the question, why do they find calculating timescales even more difficult; the answer is the same.

One approach that can be adopted is to work through a checklist of likely items that will cost the project money. Another is to assign a cost to each and every activity on the project plan – because there will be one! The best method, of course, would be to do both; thus minimising the possibility of missing things out. OK, but why, you might ask, start with estimating cost, rather than estimating timescale? Surely the plan comes first? Normally yes; but if you start with a cost model, you might be encouraged to add tasks into your plan which otherwise might have been omitted.

Consider the checklist below. Without a plan, the Project Manager will be unable to calculate some of the figures – but without the list, some significant elements might be missed from the plan. In any event, adopting an iterative approach will ensure revisiting on all fronts. It is, of course, a matter of personal preference, but the following should at least be consciously rejected:

Human Resources	**Systems Resources**	**Financial Resources**
If detailed budgeting is needed	Consumables	Accommodation
Health insurance	Depreciation	Advertising
National Insurance	Disaster recovery	Books & periodicals
Pensions	Hardware	Buildings, infrastructure & space
Salaries	Hardware accessories	Car hire
Otherwise (by work days)	Licences	Company cars
Business users	Maintenance	Conferences
IT project staff	Software	Documentation
	Telecommunications	Interview expenses
Consultants		Meals etc.
Contract IT staff		Office machinery
Other temporary staff		Photocopying
		Postage & carriage
		Protective clothing
		Stationery
		Subscriptions
		Telephone (incl. mobiles)
		Training courses
		Travel (incl. taxis, & car parking)

Perhaps not a comprehensive list, but consideration of some of these elements might well add tasks to the plan which, though necessary, would otherwise have been skipped.

Estimating timescales

Many of the disciplines relating to estimating timescales at the level of the detailed project plan are the same as those discussed earlier when considering the strategic plan. Indeed, the process flow outlined then – Key Stage Path, Key Stage Timeline, Resource Timeline, and Smoothed

Resource Timeline – could legitimately be followed. The Work Breakdown Structure (as it is commonly known) is, at this level, entirely granular and, because of this, estimates should be more accurate.

If we follow this logic through, although some of the 'givens' from Part Three still apply – such as remembering that an estimate is in fact an average – because the absolute numbers we are dealing with are that much smaller, allowances for things like contingency will be reduced too. The example used to demonstrate a method for calculating contingency later in this section demonstrates the value of working with smaller units.

Many methodologies will suggest rules for timescale estimating. 'Never create a task lasting for more than 5 days'; 'Never have more than one resource allocated to a single task'; and so on. There is no perfect answer – if there were, then all Project Managers would be using it and books on management theory would be redundant!

Young suggests that one of the most common flaws in project management is the 'insufficient effort given to getting the estimates in the first place and then subjecting them to continual review and validation.'

Keeping in mind that you will never be absolutely correct, the Project Manager needs to establish his own mantra for generating project plan estimates. This will be based on experience, consensus, gut feel, input from other people, input from other projects, recommendations, theories, and good, old-fashioned guesswork! If you need a few pointers, the following offer a reasonable start:

● Keep tasks as simple as possible:
  ➢ Try and ensure there is a 'black-and-white' outcome, so you know when they are finished.
  ➢ Keep the Task-to-Milestone ratio low: 10 to 1, not 50 to 1.
  ➢ If you have several people on a task, this should only be because they contribute differently to the accomplishment of the task, i.e. do not have two people on the same task, both of whom could be responsible for the same portion of the delivery – you won't have ownership or accountability.

> If tasks run over a long elapsed time, ask yourself if you can be certain of knowing where they are half way through the period. If you cannot, the task is wrong; change it, or break it down.

> Never assume that, if it takes one person 10 days to do a job, two people will do it in half the time. As soon as you have more than one person on the same job, communication and liaison get in the way, eating into the time allocated. There may be a management overhead too. For example:

Resources	Estimate	Communication	Management	Total
1	30	0	0	30
2	30	2	0	32
3	30	4	2	36
5	30	6	4	40

● Try, as much as possible, not to multi-thread resources; if one person is supposed to be working on three tasks simultaneously, he or she will obviously be less effective. This will be due to the inefficiency of swapping between tasks; the need to pick up where one left off; the potential inability to concentrate for appropriate periods on one single thing.

● Never schedule resources on the assumption of 100% productive effort. Use 85% as a maximum, recognising that 15% will be lost non-productive time (this is discussed in more detail in Part Five).

At the end of the process, revisit the budget – then revisit the plan. The iterative nature of this process is the constant message through this section of the book.

Of course, some people utilise estimating spreadsheets to assist them in calculating effort on individual tasks. Such an approach was most prevalent perhaps when the vast majority of programs were written using third generation languages such as COBOL. Such tools can still be applied today however, and often algorithms are developed revolving around factors such as complexity, resource experience, risk, elapsed duration etc. the result of the algorithm being used to factor up (seldom down) an original estimate. If you must use such a tool, do so only as a means of cross-checking estimates arrived at through conscious thought! Do not abdicate the development of your project plan to a spreadsheet!

Estimating Benefits

In Part Three we considered elements which, in terms of business benefit, can be used to justify strategic initiatives. To recap, we looked at such as:

- Speeding up processes
- Increasing business volumes
- Efficiency gains
- Business Process Re-organisation
- Cost Reduction.

Whichever of these may have been used as an outline justification on a project, it is prudent to revisit the assumptions made once the plan has begun to take shape. There are two fundamental reasons for doing so:

✓ Given that the Project Manager will be much closer to a more accurate estimate of the costs of the project – and that this may exceed by some degree that stated in the strategic plan – it is undoubtedly valid to cross-check costs against benefits once again.

✓ Now that the project is almost to hand, the business may want to revisit their benefit argument. It is one thing suggesting that a project might 'save' four staff, but when the project is just about to start, those 'four staff' become real people – John, Jenny, Jim and Jackie – who could conceivably be out of work within a few months. Thus, it would not be unusual to find the projected benefits reducing, particularly in cases where savings made are personnel related.

Given the two scenarios above, in the majority of cases expect the cost-benefit case to weaken as the project approaches.

'Detailed cost-benefit calculations prepared at the start of the project are worth little if they are not continually updated.'

Stephen Flowers

The final portion of this particular equation is therefore in justifying the spend outlined. This not only implies the production of a traditional Cost-Benefit model, but also defining the method by which the materialisation of projected benefits can be measured. For this reason, the project sponsor should nominate a business manager who is given the responsibility to deliver the business benefits at the end of the project; after all, one side of the equation is covered by the Project Manager who will be expected to deliver to budget – and to deliver his side of the benefits too! Failure to reap the expected benefits can destroy the validity of a project as readily as over-spend.

Ideally the benefit model can be drawn up through a simple table comparing 'as is' with 'as will be'; and it might not only be business-related benefits that are identified. In order to achieve this, there might well be a need for the business to establish a 'datum point', i.e. to measure over a representative period how it is currently performing in order to get an accurate 'as is' picture.

Consider a project to develop a new application to replace two existing systems, incorporating some revised business processes along the way. Assuming that the company in question accepts 100,000 orders per annum, the benefits argument might appear as follows:

As is	As will be	Saving	Value
It takes 100 work hours to process 200 orders	It is estimated that only 85 work hours will be needed for the same volume of orders	7,500 hours. Order entry clerks cost £6 per hour	£45,000.00
Currently, 5% of orders are entered inaccurately and need to be reprocessed	This figure is expected to fall to 2%	3,000 fewer orders will need to be re-entered. This equates to 1,500 hours	£9,000.00
Maintenance of the existing systems costs £25,000 per annum in software licence fees	These will disappear	£25,000	£25,000.00
Support for the current systems runs at 150 days per annum	The new system is expected to require only 100 days support	50 days. IT support is calculated at £200 per day	£10,000.00

This simple model gives us a benefit value of £89,000 per annum. Once the system has been implemented, some of the benefits should materialise quite quickly – order turnaround and support demands, for example – however it is insufficient to simply accept these as justifying the cost incurred by the project. The £64,000 relating to resources must manifest itself. Thus, at some point in the project documentation – and any initiation report is the logical place – a statement needs to be made in terms of how this saving will be seen. Perhaps the resource freed up will be allocated to other tasks. The productivity of the IT function might be raised slightly as a result of less support for example; or the order processing department might see its overtime bill fall. It is only when something tangible such as this happens will you know the project has actually delivered to the business – and it is precisely this kind of thing the sponsor needs to charge someone with making happen.

There will be times, of course, when the benefits will not exceed the cost. Implementation of systems projects which are seen as 'strategic' – such as a new Corporate Customer Relationship Management package – often fall into this category. Under such circumstances it is all to easy to label a project 'strategic' and in doing so make no attempt whatsoever to identify benefit. Ultimately this has to be the sponsor's call.

Before you publish

It is entirely possible that, at the commencement of the project, the manager undertook some kind of structured risk assessment in order to gain a reasonably objective indication of the likelihood of success. Let's be blunt: if he didn't undertake a risk assessment, then he certainly should have!

The 'normal' scenario in these circumstances follows this kind of pattern:

1. The Project Manager completes his risk analysis, usually in the form of a questionnaire.
2. Responses are analysed to give an overall 'score' for the project, often as a percentage – the lower the better.
3. The Project Manager makes some kind of statement about project risk in his initiation document based on the calculated score.

4. The risk analysis is filed, thrown into the back of a cupboard, and never referred to again – even when the project goes pear-shaped.

Must sound familiar! Which is a shame, as under these circumstances the Project Manager will have actually completed the bulk of the groundwork to initiate a successful risk management strategy. Perhaps if we revise the scenario a little ...

1. The Project Manager completes his risk analysis, usually in the form of a questionnaire.

   I have seen such questionnaires extend for twenty-plus pages in some of the more impractical methodologies. You should really be able to ask all the key questions on a single page of A4; indeed, this makes risk management easier.

2. Responses are analysed to give an overall 'score' for the project, often as a percentage – the lower the better.

   The score does not need to be a percentage, it could simply be the number of 'Yes' or 'No' answers given. What is important is that there is a figure that can be calculated – and later re-calculated – without interpretation, i.e. 2 plus 2 will always equal 4.

3. The Project Manager makes some kind of statement about project risk in his initiation document based on the calculated score.

   This is fine. It would be useful to state the 'score' too, and include a copy of the questionnaire in any appendix. More than this, a statement should be made in terms of how the risks identified will be managed.

4. The risk analysis is filed, thrown into the back of a cupboard, and never referred to again – even when the project goes pear-shaped. *No, no, no!*

Step 4 is obviously where the Project Manager goes wrong. Surely this is much better:

4. Based on the areas of risk identified, the Project Manager then defines the management actions that need to be undertaken. These could vary from recognition of the need to monitor, to increasing the specification of the development team's personal computers – and all points in between.

5. A risk management file is created, into which the initial questionnaire is filed along with associated management actions, and these actions become part of the Project Manager's regime (as appropriate).

6. At a predefined point in the project – at either regular intervals or logical checkpoints in the project – the risk analysis is completed again from scratch, and a new score is calculated. Steps 4 through 6 are then repeated throughout the life of the project.

There are two obvious 'wins' from this approach. Firstly, the risks are actively managed, rather than recognised then forgotten about. And secondly, by undertaking the scoring process on a regular basis, the Project Manager can map out a trend that, in most cases, would see the score reducing. This is what we would expect: as the project progresses, not only are risks being naturally eliminated (e.g. the risk that you might not get budget funding would surely have disappeared by the time you were in the implementation stage) but they should also have been 'managed out' through their explicit recognition (e.g. if more powerful PCs were purchased, then the risk we had identified diminishes radically, if not vanishing altogether).

The importance of recognising the risk management strategy now is three-fold:

1. It can be included in the project initiation phase, which can only be good practice.

2. It implies a management overhead which – however slight – you might need to take into consideration during planning, perhaps to include explicit risk assessment milestones

3. It provides a reporting mechanism that allows the business sponsors of the project to decide which risks they are prepared to take. In many cases the call should not be made by the Project Manager, particularly when addressing the risk involves 'spending' extra resource.

If focus is needed in this area, include the risk assessment score in regular reports to the project board.

Adoption of formal quality management throughout the life of a project has an impact on the initial planning stage which is not too dissimilar to risk management. An initial stance will need to be taken with respect to the programme to be followed; statements will need to be made in terms of how the programme will be managed to ensure that the desired quality is met; and there will need to be some recognition of the effort involved within the plan itself.

Whilst execution of the risk management strategy is most likely to occur as a regular element within the plan, execution of quality checks will come against specific deliverables; this will effectively add both tasks and time to the plan, which implies – at least superficially – an increase in cost. For these reasons, it may be harder to get a quality programme accepted by those who, in sponsoring the project, are interested in increasing neither timescales nor budget.

For this reason, it would be wise of the Project Manager to approach his sponsor to discuss adoption of a quality programme in advance of any detailed planning and before an initiation document is produced. A number of options could be presented, each with associated costs and potential benefits – though the latter can never be tangibly realised as they are focussed on prevention. Perhaps something along these lines would be suitable:

Measure	Cost	Benefit
Fagan's Inspections: the critical reviewing of key project documents	Probably adds one elapsed week to document sign-off; perhaps an additional 5 to 10 work days effort	Project is less likely to suffer from misunderstandings, therefore reducing time lost to rework
Production of structured and verified test plans	Probably adds up to 5 elapsed days to the development of each component to be tested, plus additional time required to carry out the tests	More robust product submitted for user acceptance; reduction in time needed for user testing will limit rework; an improved quality of product goes 'live'
Weekly team meeting to review progress against project plan	An additional weekly task, adding 'n' elapsed days to the project and costing 'n' work days effort	Quicker identification of progress issues; improved ability to monitor and adjust the project plan; improved chance of meeting defined timescales

Note: Fagan's Inspections – a process devised by Michael Fagan to proactively check and verify documentation (amongst other things) prior to its release and/or adoption in an attempt to eliminate errors, inconsistencies and ambiguities prior to that document becoming an accepted part of the project landscape, i.e. removing the causes of development error before they occur.

Obviously the kinds of measures available to the Project Manager will differ from project to project, though the 'structure' of the argument – costs against benefits – will remain the same.

It might be necessary in certain environments to attempt to quantify the benefits – 'exactly how much time will be saved in user testing?' – in order to gain maximum backing for the quality programme. A word of warning, however; do not over-sell the benefits just to get the programme accepted. Expectations will be raised, and these will need to be managed to ensure your business colleagues are not looking forward to a completely flawless implementation!

Of course, not all management fine tuning of a project plan is necessarily undertaken in an overt fashion. Indeed, it may be suggested that most hotly contested of ingredients, contingency, is an entirely invalid element used by a Project Manager to give himself an unnecessary cushion. Is contingency the Project Manager's cheat or manifestation of his realism? And if the latter – which it surely is – then perhaps being covert about its inclusion in a project plan might suggest otherwise.

For many business managers, contingency is seen an unnecessary; if the IT guys tell them something will be ready on May 1st, then that's when they will expect it – a caveat that suggests timescales might slip to the 14th is simply unacceptable. Before we look at options for including contingency in a project plan, however, perhaps a simple justification.

Ask ten people how long it will take to drive from Leeds to Manchester and you will probably get ten different answers. They might make varying assumptions in terms of exact start and end points, or base their experience on the speed at which they drive. But even if you are explicit as to precise locations and motorway speed limits, there will still be a variance. Let us assume the ten answers are as follows (in minutes):

110 120 100 120 100 120 100 115 105 110

These seem reasonable enough and lead to an average of 110 minutes. Each individual estimate is, of course, an average in itself – that is what estimates really are. If someone asks you how long you can hold your breath you might say 25 seconds; but it could be 20, or maybe

30. So 110 minutes represents an average, not a maximum. Had you asked for a maximum – and knowing the M62 and the Pennine weather – you might have arrived at a number around 300! Despite the fact that an estimate is an average, people almost always plan as if the estimate is the maximum. If we apply the kind of tolerance derived from our breath-holding example – say 20% either way – we could easily be looking at a journey which might take between 88 and 132 minutes; that's a 44 minute discrepancy, significant against an estimate of 110 minutes.

> Young asserts that 'contingencies are for the unexpected and forgotten tasks - not a safety margin to cover poor estimating of the known tasks!' While partly correct, this ignores the fact that estimates are, as we have seen, really only averages.

Your project plan is at significant risk because of the estimates it contains, no matter how good they are. Over the duration of the project, early- and late-finishing tasks may well balance themselves out – but you still have a 50% chance of going over! How's that for a justification for contingency? Surely you would like to start a project with a better than 50-50 chance of hitting the deadlines?

Thus we can argue that contingency is a valid part of the Project Manager's armoury. But how do we get it in to the plan, and how much should we aim for? You have three options for including it:

1. **Add your contingency to every task**; perhaps an additional 5% to each. This should be applied to the actual effort estimated, not the timescale. Reworking the plan with contingency added will determine new timescales; and remember, 5% additional effort will not necessarily mean that the elapsed time also increases by 5%.

2. **Add your contingency as a single lump** at the end of the project in one task. In this case you might calculate contingency based on effort, but it is probably better to inflate the elapsed time scale; if you do not add contingency to each item but to the whole, how can you predict the overall effect a slipping task will have on the actual duration of the project?

3. **Add your contingency as specific tasks** throughout the plan in a combination of 1 and 2. This is usually required when the Project Manager finds the above options are unacceptable to his business sponsor. This is when you call contingency something else, e.g. 'prototype design verification', 'network router configuration testing', and so on.

How you 'use' the contingency – i.e. when you start to book effort against it – will depend on which of the above approaches you have taken, and personal preference. How much you need will depend on the project plan itself.

As a simple illustrative example, let us assume that we have a plan that will require 500 work days of effort. Let us also assume that there is a margin of error on each task. We must remember, however, that the larger the average estimate for each task, the more likely it will be prone to error; to cater for this, we must vary these margins. We will now consider three scenarios: the first where the split between tasks finishing early/on-time/late is 60/20/20; the second 20/60/20; the third 20/20/60 (late and early tasks at the limit of their tolerance). Thus:

No of tasks	Margin of error	Average per task	Minimum per task	Maximum per task	Scenario 1 (mostly early) 60:20:20	Scenario 2 20:60:20	Scenario 3 (mostly late) 20:20:60
10	40%	50	30	70	6 x 30 = 180 2 x 50 = 100 2 x 70 = 140 **total = 420**	2 x 30 = 60 6 x 50 = 300 2 x 70 = 140 **total = 500**	2 x 30 = 60 2 x 50 = 100 6 x 70 = 420 **total = 580**
50	20%	10	8	12	30 x 8 = 240 10 x 10 = 100 10 x 12 = 120 **total = 460**	10 x 8 = 80 30 x 10 = 300 10 x 12 = 120 **total = 500**	10 x 8 = 80 10 x 10 = 100 30 x 12 = 360 **total = 540**
100	10%	5	4.5	5.5	60 x 4.5 = 270 20 x 5 = 100 20 x 5.5 = 110 **total = 480**	20 x 4.5 = 90 60 x 5 = 300 20 x 5.5 = 110 **total = 500**	20 x 4.5 = 90 20 x 5 = 100 60 x 5.5 = 330 **total = 520**

Admittedly this is a slightly artificial construct, but the table does illustrate a point of key significance. Where the average estimate is lowest – 5 work days – the potential effort range for the project is minimised; between 480 and 520 days, i.e. a variance of just 4%. Where the average estimate is the greatest – 50 work days – the potential range comes in at 420 to 580 days i.e. 16% variance. On this basis we might reasonably suggest that the level of contingency needed would be between 4% and 16%, depending on the level of detail in the plan.

This example also gives us a perfect illustration of the importance of planning to the greatest practical degree of detail. If I had to stake my career on a project, I would rather do it on one where I was reasonably confident of delivering within a 40 work day range (with contingency to cover it), rather than one where I was guessing at a 160 day range, even with contingency!

Knowing you need to use your contingency will most likely become clear when you 'spend' all the effort allocated to a task; in effect a goal has been missed. With risk management too, we might find ourselves creating targets in our plan – those regularly scheduled reviews – where once again it will become clear if they are missed. When discussing strategy, we emphasised the importance of deliverables as a means of proving progress, and this philosophy must be carried through to the project plan too. Goals – or milestones – must be set by which we can navigate.

Many Project Managers will argue that their regime of collating actual effort data and mapping this against estimated effort on a task-by-task basis – thereby to derive the percentage of task completed, and so on – is the only way of really knowing exactly where they are at any one time. This, however, falls into the trap of attempting to turn project planning into an exact science. So what if someone says – or the plan says – that a task is 85% complete and only needs another day's effort to wrap it up? Something may go wrong – perhaps an unforeseen problem, illness, or a change of requirement. The only way the Project Manager really knows the status of a task is when it is actually complete. Keep track of effort spent of course, but do not mistake this for true progress checking.

On this assumption, I must argue that the most important element of any plan – from the perspective of tracking real and tangible progress – is the milestone; a tangible delivery of something or a concrete 'happening', with a target date set against it. Milestones are imperative. Milestones equal deliverables, and a growing catalogue of deliverables equals an unequivocal proof of progress. We might even go further and suggest that a schedule of milestones – derived from a solid plan – is all you need to chart progress; and by 'progress' I mean forward motion towards the ultimate project goal.

Many methodologies will suggest progress reporting that absorbs itself in a plethora of analysis. Elements such as:

➔ number of tasks started
➔ number of tasks started to plan
➔ number of tasks started late
➔ number of tasks finished/to plan/late
➔ effort estimated to-date
➔ actual effort to-date
➔ outstanding effort
➔ planned effort on completed tasks
➔ actual effort on completed tasks
➔ effort efficiency on completed tasks
➔ projected total effort, and so on and so on …

Some of this information may be needed for budget reporting, so tracking actual effort is important, but does a range of statistics such as this actually tell anyone where the project really is? A business sponsor would most likely be bamboozled by it all, which does the IT manager no good at all in terms of credibility.

Surely a slimmer set is better; it makes progress easier to understand, and actually saves the Project Manager time! So ensure an appropriate number of milestones are set – at least 10% of tasks should result in a deliverable – and report against these. As a minimum:

➔ number of milestones due to-date
➔ number of milestones achieved to-date
➔ number of milestones achieved early or on time
➔ number of milestones outstanding.

Then list the outstanding milestones, their original planned date and current forecast date. Something as simple as this can give a better – more accurate and understandable – picture of progress than all the statistics in the world!

Our progress towards a credible progress reporting mechanism, driven by the project plan, demands something further of the Project Manager. At the outset of the project, the plan is drawn up taking into consideration all known factors pertaining at that time; assumptions, constraints and management methods should have been taken into account, and the list of deliverables/milestones defined on this basis. Obviously, as time moves on, things change – each of these most likely 'invalidating' a small part of the original plan. The following is not an usual sequence of events:

1. The Project Manager feeds weekly 'actuals' data into the plan.
2. He also adds some tasks which have recently emerged as being necessary, perhaps changing or deleting others.
3. With this new set of task and performance data, he then reschedules the plan to reflect 'today'.
4. Satisfied with this new outlook, he reports progress against the revised plan.

This is an iterative process which, usually occurring weekly, not only consumes a significant amount of time, but also takes the Project Manager further away from his starting point, i.e. that baseline against which all known criteria were defined. Most often when changing the plan, the Project Manager may not have the time or inclination to revisit assumptions, constraints, statements of scope, risk analyses and the like, and what this means is, in effect, that each week he is reporting against a new set of (undocumented) criteria. The progress report from the current week has actually had some of its links broken with the previous week – i.e. the plan has changed – and therefore comparative analysis (we have or have not improved) actually becomes impossible. Many Project Managers actually work this way in order to massage the message, continually attempting to deliver the best gloss possible on their project.

Such an approach has to be wrong both morally and technically. The only way to truly gauge progress is to do so with a standard set of measures – and against a consistent datum. In project planning parlance, use of the baseline is often ignored by Project Managers; either they do not set one at the beginning of the project, or they change it each time they modify their plan. This is crazy! So some rules:

Rule 1. When you have a complete and signed-off project plan, set the baseline. Undoubtedly you will be using some kind of tool for this – such as Microsoft's 'Project' – and setting a baseline can be as simple as pressing a button!

Rule 2. Always report progress against the fixed point represented by the baseline; this is the only way to know where you are against your original ambition. Remember, this fixed point will equate not only to timescale but also resource, effort and budget.

Rule 3. Change the baseline at your peril! Doing so – unless absolutely justified – will not make the project any more successful.

Of course, circumstances may arise where it becomes positively misleading to report against an original baseline. Typically a major re-scoping of the project with a significant change in the end goals or deliverables would warrant such a move; perhaps an extra three business locations have been added to your remit, or you now need to take into consideration additional requirements from another four user departments. Change the plan, get the new version agreed, then re-baseline – but do not forget that you should also revisit all elements of the datum plan including risks, assumptions etc. After all, you are effectively beginning a new project.

Milestones and the Project Baseline; <u>real</u> project management tools!

Final elements of the plan

As with the process defined to put together a strategic plan, there is a solid argument to pause and take stock – especially when you believe that you have a 'finished' project plan. Call it part of your quality management programme if you like, but a review – hopefully carried out with peers or senior team members – has to make sense. There are also some particular project considerations which warrant a second glance: the impact of interfaces; multi-site implementations; recovery and backup; demands of subsequent maintenance; and non-productive time. We recognised some of these earlier to ensure we had considered their impact at a strategic level, and their importance should be recognised through our planning work.

Interfacing, as we have already said, brings with it issues relating to general resource need, the dependence on others, and additional layers of complexity (see Part Three). More than this, the project plan needs to ensure that such things are explicitly catered for. In the normal scheme of things, the particular initiative the Project Manager is working on might require application data interfaces (typically) with other systems – systems over which the manager concerned might have no control. In addition to defining the tasks required to build these interfaces, the manager must ensure not only that appropriate milestones exist to cover the work on his project, but also that these are accepted by other teams, internal or external, who are required to execute against the same plan.

I would suggest that 'normal' milestones are inadequate under these circumstances. If any portion of the development is out of your control, then increase the number of milestones – and, if possible, deliverables – in order to give yourself the best possible chance of managing this aspect of the project. Not only that, but such an approach also gives the Project Manager the ability to address the additional complexity he is set to face. Consider the basic comparison opposite where we look at 'simple' module against a dual-update, interface development.

In this example, the effect on our project of needing to develop a multi-system interface can be clearly seen. We have moved from 10 milestones to 25; and out of these, there are 15 (those in italics) over which the project manage has, at best, only partial control.

Undoubtedly this is a risk to be managed, and the benefit of having more agreed milestones to keep track of the work is self-evident. It is also interesting to contemplate how, if we adopted the 'consistent interface' approach advocated when discussing this subject in Part Three, the number of milestones would be closer to 10 than 25, with the vast majority still within the Project Manager's control.

As with external interfaces, dealing with multi-site roll-outs of a single 'system' – from many locations in a single country to several sites in any number of countries – should similarly increase the number of milestones the Project Manager needs to identify. The equation is more involved than simply assuming that two locations

	'Simple'	Interface
PLANNING	• Define all tasks/milestones in project plan	• Define all tasks/milestones in project plan • Define all tasks/milestones in secondary project plan • Cross-check all milestone dates to ensure fit
DEVELOPMENT	• Complete module specification • Complete development of module	• Complete module specification • Complete module specification in secondary system • Verify the functional fit between specifications • Complete development of module • Complete development of module in secondary system
TESTING	• Define unit test/system plan • Complete unit test of module	• Define unit test/system plan • Define unit test/system plan in secondary system • Define integration test plan between systems • Complete unit test of module • Complete unit test of module in secondary system • Complete integration testing between systems
USER ACCEPTANCE	• Define acceptance test plan • Complete user acceptance testing • Gain user sign-off of module	• Define acceptance test plan • Define acceptance test plan in secondary system • Define acceptance test plan for interface processing • Complete user acceptance testing • Complete user acceptance testing in secondary system • Complete user acceptance testing of the interface processing • Gain user sign-off of module • Gain user sign-off of module in secondary system • Gain user sign-off of interface processing
IMPLEMENTATION	• Define implementation plan • Implement module into 'live' system	• Define implementation plan • Define implementation plan in secondary system • Implement module into both 'live' systems simultaneously

means twice as many milestones, as the interface example above has demonstrated. But in addition to any 'extra' physical deliverables, the Project Manager has other issues to consider which need to be recognised now in order to prevent compromising the plan.

Unlike the interface scenario where the other end of the handshake is almost peripheral to the main objective of the project, the multi-site roll-out is actually integral to the whole project goal. This implies that the Project Manager may need to extend the range of his management brief to include these additional sites; certainly this is true in the following circumstances:

- the satellite location is developing part of the overall solution, e.g. in a shared development situation
- the satellite location is developing its own specific portion of the final solution, e.g. in terms of 'localisation' for a multi-national application development project or package implementation
- where the satellite location's systems environment is sufficiently different to warrant a modified or enhanced technical solution, e.g. delivering into a remote Novell site, where the main centre runs Windows NT.

There are obviously many more potential examples. Whatever the situation, such complexity demands the Project Manager ask some fundamental questions:

- **?** Is there a need for separate, local project plans – and if so, how is the overall managed?
- **?** Is there a need for a local project budget – and if so, how are these aggregated for tracking?
- **?** Are there resource implications in terms of other locations needing call on 'core' staff?
- **?** Are there sufficient business resources available across all sites?
- **?** What is the impact of any differing working or business practices? – particularly relevant in multi-national situations from a legal perspective
- **?** Are there issues in terms of co-ordinating the implementation, particularly in relation to the 'go live' date?
- **?** Are there time zone issues – and if so, what is the impact on support?

? If a software development, are there knock-on effects in terms of network traffic?

? What impact will the development have on any disaster recovery plan?

Again, a summary of potential issues, but sufficient to see that the Project Manager may need to add more milestones to his plan at the very least – if not, as in the case of disaster recovery or network bandwidth, entirely new sections. More than this, there are significant additional management issues to ensure successful cross-site co-ordination, collaboration and support. This implies a much larger management pool and potentially an impact on project organisation. Such considerations also raise questions in terms of authority and responsibility; additional clarity will be required in terms of management scope, and reporting lines will need to be explicitly drawn and agreed – again, especially with multi-cultural work.

If, after consideration of the kind of factors outlined above, the Project Manager revisits and enhances his overall plan – perhaps even developing sub-plans for the various locations – then he must also revisit any other work carried out thus far to identify similar impact. Risk management and contingency calculations are obvious examples. I suggest that it is inevitable that the Project Manager will not address all pertinent issues – practical and political – in the first cut of his project plan, and that re-working the plan – along with risks, contingency, disaster recovery, support et al – is also an inevitability.

Recovery and backup is, quite simply, one element of the systems infrastructure most often overlooked or relegated to the bottom of the priority pile. Under normal circumstances, the disaster recovery plan is something which is dusted off on an annual basis – and possibly tested even less. In many environments this may well be a valid approach; and for many new projects or initiatives, there will be no impact on the procedures already in place. However – and here is the greatest flaw – the vast majority of projects are put together without any consideration of the potential impact on the existing disaster recovery schema at all, and in failing to do so, the whole enterprise, not just the individual single project, may be placed in jeopardy.

By definition, virtually any project will change the existing systems infrastructure, usually adding something new; a server perhaps, new network equipment, new software, or simply more data. If the Project Manager is adding components in this way, then the overall pot of systems resource is increasing, and therefore the demands on any disaster recovery schematic must also increase. Imagine what would happen if a new project doubled the volume of data within an application system or an upgrade required a more powerful AS/400 – and the emergency back-up plan failed to provide sufficient disc capacity or processing power. The disaster recovery plan becomes a disaster in itself!

The message is a simple one: consider the impact of the changes the project will make to the overall infrastructure with respect to the disaster recovery plan. If the backup regime needs to be changed to accommodate this, then plan to do so. You must factor the work – and its cost – into your project plan because it has arisen as a direct result of your project. Do not assume that you will be able to pick up the cost at some later time either; an adequate disaster recovery plan needs to be in place when the project goes 'live', not six months later. And when changes to the disaster backup plan are made, plan to test them too; signing a contract with your supplier on the basis of a promise that they will be able to accommodate your increased demand should not be enough. After all, disaster recovery is a business function and should be signed off in the same way as any other.

In a similar way to disaster recovery considerations, the Project Manager needs to spend some of his attention on the future, particularly with respect to the ongoing maintenance overhead to which his project may be adding. The most obvious example of this is where the project involves the implementation of a modified commercial business application package. Indeed, we have already alluded to the cost of such as being not only the immediate change but also retro-actively fitting – and re-testing – of any changes made in future releases of the software. A willy-nilly approach to such bespoke enhancements can actually undermine a cost-benefit case for the project as a whole, if not negate it completely!

Of course, unless one is very lucky, 'vanilla' is pretty much an impossibility. Accepting this, it would be prudent for the Project Manager to define his approach to modification and enhancement up-front – particularly with respect to the maintenance spiral he may be in danger of creating. One approach, of course, is to be particularly rigorous in getting approval for changes required to any base package. Indeed, this method – often embarked upon by the Project Manager with the most sincere intention of actually preventing change – is most often than not over-ridden by the business whose need for changes in system functionality are paramount. One modification leads to ten, ten to twenty, and so on. Vanilla is replaced by Raspberry Ripple.

One alternative approach is to allow enhancement, but rather than accept changes to the base package, implement these as separate additional modules that can be 'plugged in', hopefully leaving the base package largely untouched.

If, for example, additional function is required to allow interactive cross-referencing between orders and an overall business summary for a customer, rather than enhance any base package order processing modules, why not provide a hook into a custom module which does the job? If this has the same 'look and feel' of the package, will any user notice or care? And when it comes to any upgrade, the 'hook' may be all that needs to be retro-fitted and tested. Of course, this approach will not work in every single case, but it does gives the Project Manager a fighting chance of not compromising the viability of his project too much!

Dotting the 'i's

So, now you have a plan complete with all the elements outlined above – but what do you do with it next? And what happens when the work actually starts?

Before you unleash your plan on an unsuspecting world, there is one final thing to ensure you have covered; unproductive time. How many Project Managers generate an 8 hour-a-day, 5 day-a-week work schedule only to find themselves inexorably slipping behind for no immediately apparent reason? No-one is productive all the time, whatever their intention. Holidays, sickness, training, administration and management overheads all conspire to deflect and dilute resources. The Project Manager needs to recognise – and account for

– this non-productive time up-front, and factor it into the plan to help ensure viability of his schedule.

How much time is non-productive? Over many years and many projects, I have been surprised to find that consistently around 15% is lost. Typically people will have 20 to 25 days annual leave – which is already around 10% of available working days. There will be some sickness somewhere, and following the project procedures, processes and methods will incur something in the way of administration on a weekly if not daily basis. So allow 15%. Don't cut it – because you can't! – and ensure you track against it. Have holidays, sickness, admin etc. as specific tasks with all resources allocated to them, then record accumulated time against each. Keep an eye on any 'admin' bucket though, as this is the one most likely to be abused. You may discover some people claiming a day a week in 'admin' or – worse still! – 'management'. Find out what they meant by making such a recording: they might not understand the system, or simply be poor (or lazy) recorders of their own time. Alternatively, they might effectively only be working four days a week! Visibility gives the Project Manager a chance to correct such anomalies; it also gives him the chance to adjust his own process demands if he finds that the project regimen is forcing a 10% admin overhead on everyone, every week.

The subject of keeping track is one we will consider in greater detail in Part Five, but a note is worthwhile now. Having developed the project plan, the Project Manager needs to be clear exactly how he will record facts – what has happened – against his schedule. A traditional model would suggest detailed time recording with the data accumulated against tasks in the plan. Project planning tools allow this to be accomplished to varying degrees of sophistication of course, but one mistake often made arises from errant philosophy; namely, the belief that the plan is fundamentally a definition of reality. In this model, the Project Manager might be seen every Monday spending hours entering data into his Microsoft Project or Project Manager Workbench plan – then even more hours adjusting and tinkering in a futile attempt to reflect the world.

The Project Manager needs to ask himself three key questions:

? **How much detail is really useful?** This should already be reflected in the way the plan looks. If there is redundancy in the plan, at whatever level, then the management overhead will be unnecessarily large.

? What does the Project Manager need to enable him to manage? An example would be enough non-productive 'buckets' to allow him to keep effective track – not so many as to make recording time confusing and analysis impossible.

? What does the business want? Almost certainly the project's sponsor will not want to see a detailed Gantt chart; but they are likely to want updates at a certain level – breadth and depth – and this information should be easily derived or assembled from the plan and the data recorded within it.

By answering these three questions, the Project Manager is able to undertake a last-minute sanity check on his plan. Is the level of detail correct? Will the regular data/effort/completion recording regimen capture the critical information needed by both himself and the business? Is the plan in danger of becoming a burden to the Project Manager to manage, to the team to support, and to the business to understand? The key aim must be to eliminate unnecessary and unproductive management; to work smarter.

And finally we have it: a project plan which covers all necessary elements and facets of the project; a project plan based on solid and documented foundations; a project plan with sound realistic estimates, recognising the need for contingency and the impact of non-productive time.

Time to sound the alarum? Nearly. One last cross-check of the detail in the plan against budget and cost; perhaps, if you have the time, a final walkthrough with senior members of the team. Remember, the plan and all it represents – budget, organisation etc. – is a nailing of one's colours to the mast. The Project Manager should be presenting a coherent and cohesive package he believes in; not, as is often the case, a rough Gantt chart knocked-up over lunchtime. In many instances the project plan will act as the key tool in selling the project to the business. If the architect you commissioned to build your dream house said, 'Plans? Look, I've done dozens of these! There'll be four bedrooms, just like you said, and a south-facing conservatory. All I need is £250,000 and we'll get started,' I suspect you might just be a little wary ...

So, the plan is published and the business is on-board. Communicate the start date to all those for whom it is relevant; then communicate any rules, processes and procedures that will apply for the duration of the project to those who need to know. The latter may appear to be mainly administration, but you and the people working with you need to be clear on how and when they record time, how holidays are booked, how they process a user's request for change, how to initiate spend against the budget, how to request additional resource and so on.

Are all the 't's crossed and the 'i's dotted? It may have taken longer than you had first imagined, but you, your team and the business will have arrived on the starting blocks with the best possible chance of success. Remember, others might have got away two or three weeks before you – but there's a better than even chance that these will also be the people who would finish two or three months later than they had predicted.

And now all you have to do is fire the starting pistol!

5

Project Management

Some project management basics

At the commencement of any project – from that moment when the trigger of the metaphorical starting pistol is pulled – the Project Manager needs to be clear in his own mind how he will handle a number of key issues should they arise. The project plan, however carefully crafted and developed during the previous days or weeks, becomes his map by which to navigate through the implementation jungle. Make no mistake, it is nothing more. Any illusion that a solid plan is the nirvana of project management needs to be dispelled, despite the emphasis that has been placed upon it thus far. If the plan is the map, then management skills represent the compass. Give the poor manager a good plan and he will still probably fail; give a good manager a poor plan, and there will still be some chance of success.

We aim, of course, for good plans and good managers!

Clarity at the outset is aided by the Project Manager understanding how he will address a number of key issues: lack of authority; user apathy; erosion of principles; communication; and response to mistakes.

Lack of authority

In Part Two, we began our consideration of the imbalance likely between responsibility and authority, and the problems that this can present to the Project Manager. We also suggested ways in which this might be addressed. By the time the Project Manager reaches the practical commencement of his project, he should have formalised much in terms of the process for bridging this gap. Moreover, he should also have established an understanding of where the political power base resides in the organisation – particularly with respect to his own project – and he should have an unclouded view of those who represent his most powerful supporters and allies.

None of this second element will be documented; nor should it be. Such an appreciation is pure politics; the ability to manage people to your benefit. Often, of course, effective proponents in this area are seen as devious, and the term 'hidden agenda' is not uncommonly used to suggest almost Machiavellian intent. Play this game well and the Project Manager can often ensure confidence is maintained, support forthcoming, and influence with sponsors and other budget- and resource-holders kept positive.

The bottom line is that we are talking about people management – and the 'management' of peers and superiors often within the business community. Keep these supporters involved and informed; make them feel that their contribution is important and valued; endeavour to ensure that there is something in the project for them. The poor manager may regard this advice as pandering to vanity. The good manager will do it well and maintain a high personal regard – and project support – even when things get a little rocky.

User apathy

Of course, if the Project Manager is successful in pursuing a prudent and fruitful 'hidden agenda' of his own, he may be well on the way to nullifying the negative potential impact of user apathy. This distraction most likely manifests itself in the business failing to provide appropriate resource at key stages of the project – requirements definition or acceptance testing – on the basis of resources being too busy and the project being something that belongs to the IT world.

We have already stressed how any IT plan is a business plan, and that a significant portion of the Project Manager's skill lies in getting this message accepted. The ideal is to work in an environment with a supportive, committed and responsibility-sharing user community – but what if this is not the case? What if there is apathy and an unwillingness to commit? Style may have an effect here. The straight-talking Project Manager may feel that a direct approach is required;

but often this bluntness leads to misinterpretation and confrontation. A softer approach can often fail because those whose support is needed prove to be politically stronger, or more ruthless, or manipulative. Playing Mr Nice Guy can sometimes deliver nothing.

In both these extreme examples, perception and the subjective view can dominate and derail. By the time the project starts, the Project Manager should have a sense of the apathy issue – and arm himself accordingly with an approach that is objective, factual and demonstrable. But how?

The key tool is to include 'business only' milestones in the plan; deliverables upon which the project is dependent in order to move forward in accordance with the delivery schedule. Make sure the business community is clearly aware of these up-front, and if there is a danger that they will be missed, ensure your reporting mechanism includes milestones and the impact on the project in terms of timescale slippage or cost. If the project sponsor is doing his job properly – and particularly if he is one of the project's key supporters – the Manager should have a decent chance of getting a positive resolution.

Of course, apathy can come from other areas too, such as sister IT organisations or departments, or those located in other cities or countries. The same approach – to deliver clear and indisputable factual evidence – is the Project Manager's best weapon.

Erosion of principles

In both of these areas – authority and apathy – the Project Manager's personal standing can have a significant influence on whether issues arise in the first place and also how quickly they get resolved.

We have talked about defining the processes and rules by which the project will be run, and about how any initiation report represents nailing your colours to the project mast. We have suggested that the Project Manager needs to be true to himself, promising to deliver only what he knows can be delivered. Such platitudes may sound trite, but they are important. If as Project Manager you define an approach, processes, rules, or methods then stick to them. Failure to deliver even small things can erode confidence. If you have undertaken to deliver a weekly newsletter on your project, but after a month it has died a death, what conclusions might potential detractors draw about your ability to manage the overall project? Conversely, if you have undertaken to deliver X, Y, and Z, and you consistently do so, then you are more likely to be respected for your management ability and integrity – which will have positive benefits elsewhere. If this means some tough talking occasionally and being prepared to stick your neck out, then be prepared to do so; your stock will rise.

Of course this is not to say that you cannot make changes in any processes you have set-up. But if you do need to, make changes in a visibly managed way with solid reasons and benefits. Do not shirk or hide from such situations. And if you make a poor call, put your hand up and acknowledge it. Being honest – and being prepared to act – can also earn respect.

Communication

Too little or too much? More often than not, the Project Manager is guilty of the former. Even more often, however, he is guilty of providing poor quality communication to the project's stakeholders. This isn't to say that the base information disseminated is incorrect, but rather the means of delivery is flawed.

Setting up a communication channel to report project progress can prove to be something of a mine field; which is perhaps rather a surprise given both its nature and the fact that it is divorced from the key deliverable of the project itself. So where might we detect these mines – i.e. what blows us out of the water?

- **'Asking the user community what they want to see.'** It is likely that they will not really know; and if opinions are expressed, the Project Manager might find himself attempting to pander to widely differing demands, and consequently wasting time in putting them together. The only person the Project Manager should consult is the project's sponsor.

- **'Providing stakeholders with an exact copy of what the Project Manager needs to see.'** Network diagrams and Gantt charts will tell the user community nothing – because of the interpretation issue – and will only serve to alienate. Recognise those things that are important to the key non-IT players – usually delivery dates and budget performance – and build around that.

💣 **'Utilising a given report from project management software on the assumption that it is an accepted standard.'** It isn't. Take the data (if the data is relevant) and incorporate it into a format that is easily digestible for business partners.

💣 **'Embarking on an over-ambitious publicity programme** – the fortnightly newsletter – which is both difficult to maintain and unlikely to be read by its intended audience after issue number 3.' Go large and glossy at important moments during the project – commencement, development completion, launch – but only then, because those are the times when you really have something to say.

There are a number of critical success factors for the Project Manager in this area.

- Keep the information consistent.
- Ensure the information is of good quality – i.e. has a sound basis in fact, not fiction or opinion.
- Ensure any communication is regular.
- Make the format concise and easy to digest in two minutes – make it easy to produce too!
- Ensure that data is accessible and not requiring hours to calculate or create.

Rocket science this isn't, so there should never be any acceptable excuse for getting it wrong. Think about the qualities you might associate with your bank statement.

- It's timely – monthly makes sense.
- It's concise – usually only a page or two (unless you've just won the lottery).
- It contains all the information you need: payees, amounts, balance.
- You can choose to scan it quickly, or use it to cross-check against other records.

If you think of your project's progress report as being equivalent to its bank statement, you won't go far wrong.

Response to mistakes

No-one is perfect. Even the Project Manager with years of multi-million dollar projects behind him will slip up occasionally. So it will be with the project team: there will be errors of judgement; quality will not be 100%; estimates will be wrong. The Project Manager needs to have a positive attitude to such circumstances. Without doubt, he will need his team to show initiative and to take risks occasionally; indeed, they may need to be encouraged to do so in order to keep the project rattling along.

In this world of continuous decision-making – and therefore risk-taking – the Project Manager needs to encourage and not stifle. This means being prepared to deal with issues created by errors and mistakes, supporting the team as they work through the project. This may sound bland, but many projects – often those driven 'by the book' – generate a blame culture that prohibits those little leaps that propel the project forwards.

Obviously there will be some transgressions which will not be acceptable, and these usually fall into a category that might be labelled 'unprofessional': the blatant failure to adhere to procedures; the inappropriate attitude towards colleagues, peers and users; failure to meet standards set by the overall organisation – most obviously in terms of time-keeping or dress code. In as much as it is important for the Project Manager to be seen to be supportive, it is also vital that he is seen to deal promptly with these more difficult issues. Respect is perhaps the greatest accolade a Project Manager can hope to achieve.

The value of tools

When faced with the trials and tribulations of project management, many organisations look to adopt tools to provide them with additional support in an endeavour to give the best opportunity for success. Generically, these tend to fall into two camps; Project Management Methodologies, and Project Management Software. Despite the hype that accompanies some, methodologies are no God-given project management solution. There is no guarantee that adopting Prince 2 – for example – will ensure success any more than other similar approaches. It is reasonable to say, however, that the absence of a methodology – be it industry standard or locally and personally defined – may well prove a hindrance to successful delivery.

Broadly speaking, methodologies offer a structure; a set of rules and processes which help the Project Manager to bring a sense of order to an otherwise chaotic world. Despite this positive press, we must also recognise that, in the wrong environment, they might either breed masses of forms and unnecessary overheads, turning project management into little more than an expensive paper chase, or else fall woefully short of stringent project demands. Whichever method is employed, it is important that it is aligned to fit the project. Adopting full-scale Prince 2 methodology on a six-week internet-related project, for example, could well result in extending the timescale of the project simply for the sake of the methodology, not for the good of the project. The truism is that the Project Manager needs to define a set of processes that are appropriate for the project; a package implementation requires very different control from a strategy definition project.

The vast majority of Project Managers attain their lofty position after considerable exposure to projects through more varying roles. It is also likely that they will have a satchel of experiences which given them a reasonable view as to the kinds of methods with do and do not work for them. In many respects, any project management methodology is a collation of such tools – based upon individuals' experience and common sense – brought together as a single, cohesive whole. On this basis, there is no reason why the astute and capable Project Manager should not be able to define his own super- or sub-set – should the need arise – based on one or more existing methodologies.

Often Project Managers will find themselves with a range of projects that need to be managed simultaneously, and often these projects are of varying size. One useful approach here is to (a) define the super-set to be used on the largest of projects, then (b) define sub-sets for 'smaller' endeavours. From this, a checklist can be drawn up which provides an appropriately sized mechanism for each project without compromising the overall methodology. For example:

Element	Large	Medium	Small
Project Definition Document	Yes	Yes	Yes
Risk Analysis	Yes	Yes	Possibly
Issue Management Procedure	Yes	Possibly	Possibly
Project Board/Steering Committee	Yes	Possibly	No
Adoption of horizon planning techniques	Yes	Possibly	No
Formal Change Management Process	Yes	Possibly	Possibly
... and so on			

The advantage of having this matrix-based approach is that you need define elements of the methodology only once, and are then free to pick and choose as appropriate to each project. Whichever combination is chosen, the Project Manager has a reasonable chance of ensuring a supportive framework which will act as a cohesive whole, i.e. the consistency defined across the complete suite of tools should apply across any sub-set. What constitutes 'large' or 'small' will undoubtedly be organisation-dependant.

Having defined the set of activities or tasks required to complete the entire project or project phase, the Project Manager often turns to his software-based project management tool. Translating a work breakdown structure into graphical form has the advantage of providing a more readily assimilated overview of project status, with the software itself offering a mechanism to track progress, time, dependencies and so on. Unfortunately for many, such tools – Microsoft Project, Project Manager Workbench, SuperProject Expert – are adopted as a panacea for good project control, effectively abdicating the essence of management. Like a methodology, it is important to recognise that the tools themselves guarantee nothing; it is their contribution to an overall management regime that is important.

So are such tools worth the trouble, and what value do they provide? Provided they are not slavishly used in pursuit of an image of reality, the answer to the first part is more 'yes' than 'no'. Provided they are pragmatically used as communication tool – primarily as an early warning device for the Project Manager – then they do offer benefit. Take an elapsed task over ten days, with two resources allocated. After the first four days, Resource A has already spent 3 days of his planned 6; Resource B, 4 days from 7. The task is estimated as 55% complete. Is the task ahead of schedule or not? And will completing the remainder of the task impact on resource commitment elsewhere? If the answer is not immediately obvious, isn't a tool that automatically turns such tasks 'red' worth having?

What is not worth having is the monster schedule that requires all of Monday to input the previous week's data, with subsequent tweaks to resource allocation and end-dates. Despite popular belief, this isn't Project Management.

A third tool – and one that is woefully under-utilised – is the 'audit'. Primarily through negative connotations and the negative impact accountants are perceived to have on projects, this has become something of a dirty word. However, a constructive external view can provide a valuable sanity check at almost any stage of a project. It is not only large organisations with dedicated departments who should consider the value of the voluntary – and involuntary! – audit; given the right parameters and outline, a short, peer-based audit can prove invaluable.

How might this work? Perhaps the IT organisation is large enough to be running three projects of varying sizes concurrently. Let us assume that they are more or less adhering to an agreed methodology for the company, with local variations driven by project size etc. Given that each of these projects' managers should have a similar view of how each project should be structured (from a management perspective) peer-based auditing should be easy.

1. Provide a copy of the Project Initiation Report, plus all backup material.
2. Define where there might be deviations from any corporate or departmental standard.
3. Provide access to up-to-date plans and other documentation – such as risk and issue logs.
4. Define the required output from the audit, with a slant towards anything the Project Manager is particularly concerned about.
5. Provide access to project team members and the user community.
6. Await the output!

There is no reason why, after little more than a week, a summary health check should not be available for the Project Manager. Most things should be running well, but there may be some things the manager has become too close to, and where they are unable to recognise both real issues and potential solutions. For limited cost, the Project Manager might find himself with some positive suggestions in terms of his management strategy – i.e. things he could usefully do, or stop doing – and the existence of the 'external' report should hopefully give the user community confidence in the way the project is being run. In this peer-to-peer environment, the fact that the Project Manager might be scrutinising the auditor's own project in a few weeks, should help engender a positive and co-operative spirit!

If peer auditing is not an option – and there is no internal audit function – then consider a truly external audit from an independent consultancy. This will cost money – of course! – but might well save in the long term. Showing a willingness to put this kind of quality check into the project management process can only help establish and maintain credibility within the user community. Whichever approach is taken, the same old rules apply: allow for the work in the budget, and allow for the tasks in the plan.

The perils of change

One of the greatest enemies faced by the Project Manager – some would argue the greatest – is the phenomenon commonly known as 'Scope Creep'. What is scope creep? How do we define and recognise it? And how do we manage it?

The words, not unnaturally, give us the definition. We are talking about the situation where, having defined something within particular parameters – the 'scope' part – we find ourselves dealing outside of the box that had been so carefully defined – the 'creep'. Scope creep is usually – but not entirely – associated with non-IT personnel within a project, and the typical reaction is that such people are vilified and plagues are begged to be set upon them. However, the phenomenon the Project Manager is forced to manage is entirely natural; indeed, he himself is almost certainly guilty of it in everyday life.

Take a trip to the supermarket. Often this is undertaken with a list – the scope – and almost always the purchaser leaves with a few things in their basket they had not planned on buying – the 'creep'. Perhaps you are buying a new car and have a defined budget in mind (scope); how many of us would not be prepared to stretch that budget a little (creep) for the sake of alloy wheels, metallic paint, or high-specification stereo?

The IT project is no different. The shopping list is the requirements definition document; the extra groceries are the bells and whistles asked for once the prototype has been seen.

'Change is an inevitable consequence of moving through time.'

Baker & Baker

This must apply at all levels, from the strategic to the detailed plan. Another argument, therefore, for regular strategy reviews (see Part Six).

The problem for the Project Manager is that scope creep has an immediate impact on the project plan; and this impact is most often realised in terms of end-date slippage, and a rise in the overall cost of the project. Change is therefore seen as the enemy. But it is important to recognise two things. One, the IT project itself is about change; and two, it is therefore only uncontrolled change which is the problem (the project plan should, after all, represent change that is being controlled). The Project Manager needs, therefore, tools to turn uncontrolled change into controlled change. He also needs to recognised the time to call those tools into action – and this is at the very first sighting of the enemy.

Of course, preparations for the battle are made well in advance. By the time the Project Manager puts together his Project Initiation Report he should already have at least three of his troops mustered, namely his risk management strategy, his issue management strategy, and his change management strategy. Why might they be needed so early? Because risks and issues will materialise as he is about to put pen to paper – and change the moment after!

Risk and issue management

The most common mistake made in attempting this kind of management is that, after significant up-front effort in defining the risks or issues a project faces, nothing further is done. Remember our views on the use of constraints or assumptions? Risk and issue management is no different. Define the risks, certainly, but also state how they will be managed, i.e. what you will do to prevent their occurrence and stop them being risks.

Before going further, I should perhaps define the difference in these terms which, like assumption and constraint, are often muddled or misinterpreted:

➜ **Risk:** 'the possibility of incurring misfortune or loss' (Hanks, Ed. 1979, p1259). Something that has the potential to happen, thereby creating uncontrolled – i.e. unplanned – change.

➜ **Issue:** 'an important subject requiring a decision' (Hanks, Ed. 1979, p776). Where a failure to obtain a decision may create uncontrolled change; typically this might be a delay in deciding business direction or something relating to project staffing or funding.

It is important that we recognise each of these as agents of change that are initially out of our control. Having a management strategy is all about keeping them within our control.

During Part Four, we talked about a risk management approach which endeavoured to offer the Project Manager a 'score' by which the health of the project – its 'riskiness' – could be regularly measured. More common is the approach which defines a log in more of a 'free form'. Nowadays, this log can easily be automated via a PC database, the idea being that when a risk or issue arises, this is noted and – hopefully – action taken or scheduled. For either risk or issue, the data held is pretty much the same. As a minimum:

➜ some kind of reference number
➜ title and description
➜ priority
➜ date entry was raised and the person who raised the risk/issue
➜ status i.e. open, in progress, on hold, closed
➜ action to be taken and the person charged with taking that action
➜ date the entry is to be reviewed.

The last two points are key. Unless action is to be taken, there is no point in keeping the log – on its own, it would just become a list and not a management tool. Similarly, unless open risks and issues are reviewed and revisited – until they have gone away – they are simply not being managed. Formally review risk or issues logs (if you choose to incorporate them into your project) either weekly, fortnightly or monthly, depending on the type and duration of the project. These reviews should include key players from across the project; it may be necessary to raise the priority of an entry in order to force action, and this is a business decision. It may sound a little simplistic, but by the time the project comes to an end, there should be no open risks or issues remaining.

We have already considered aspects of quality management when looking at project planning, and obviously risk and issue management strategies – if implemented – represent further examples of how the Project Manager might choose to infuse his project with quality safeguards. If choosing to adopt any kind of risk or issue management strategy, the same ground rules apply as before: only promise what you can practically deliver, and include the regular review tasks into the plan to ensure they are not forgotten.

How the Project Manager chooses to act in response to the changes that assail his project – be they 'scope creep' or the impacts of risks or issues – we will address in our next section...

Where are we?

In many respects, consideration of where a project 'is' at any stage in its life defines much of what project management is really all about. The ability to answer the question, 'where are we?' at any point in time is largely derived from a set of constant activities which revolve around monitoring and reporting, and which focus – in all but the smallest of cases – in where we are against a plan. Indeed, given that any project plan represents a road map of change – and that diversions along the way are effectively additional changes (hopefully controlled!) on top of that already identified – it could be argued that the Project Manager is also a change manager.

Management may well be 'the technique, practice, or science of managing or controlling' and 'the skilful or resourceful use of materials, time etc.' (Hanks, Ed. 1979, p894), but it is also about being able to co-ordinate change in a controlled fashion. So, in the progress from A to B, the question 'where are we?' is key, and hence the Project Manager's road should be punctuated with processes and reviews (not all necessarily formal) which are focussed on understanding the project's current position in an arena of change.

This management skill manifests itself most obviously in (a) monitoring the health of the project against parameters of time, resource and budget, (b) ensuring that all change is controlled, and (c) in the demonstration – through project reporting – that nothing is unmanaged. Things may be late perhaps, or there may be alterations in the delivery schedule, but nothing is unmanaged. Given that what and how the Project Manager reports is the clearest indication of this state – or not! – then the importance of these reports is obvious.

To a certain extent, the exact format of the Project Manager's progress report is unimportant, and it would be ludicrous to define any 'ideal' blueprint here. We might suggest that it be succinct, factual and objective, but to go further would be spurious. What we do need to consider, however, is how the Project Manager can put himself into a position to both provide an informative, accurate and quality progress report, and how he goes about turning the uncontrolled event into managed change.

In order to be certain that project reporting is entirely consistent throughout the duration of the project, it is vital that the manager concentrates on the facts. If we forget the plan itself for a moment, we have already identified a number of additional tangible measures:

- risk analysis – a 'score' which is consistently applied throughout the project's life
- risks and issues – total number and then broken down by status e.g. open, closed
- changes – total number, impact in terms of time or budget
- quality management – e.g. output statistics from Fagan inspections

If we then add in key metrics from the plan itself, we see how much factual data the Project Manager has to play with:

- milestones/deliverables – e.g. total hit; % hit early, % hit late; outstanding
- effort – e.g. total effort to-date; expected effort to-date; outstanding effort; revised estimate
- cost – e.g. total cost to-date; expected cost to-date; outstanding cost; revised cost estimate

There are a myriad potential combinations here – which is one reason why I chose not to suggest any 'ideal' format – and certainly enough to report progress on a consistent basis.

Simply listing a whole raft of numeric values is entirely insufficient of course. The data will need interpretation, and this should be carried out objectively; subjective statements are essentially meaningless in the project environment, defying interpretation and impossible to manage. One trap into which Project Managers often fall, however, is not only in the failure to interpret the data objectively, but also in their missing the key messages that can be unearthed through the recognition of trends.

When talking about risk analysis, we have already stated that our risk 'score' should reduce over time. Checking that this is the case is an example of simple trend analysis. If we go further, however, and relate the data in our progress report to that from the previous weeks or months, consider what greater depth of management information we can unearth! So the message is 'measure, measure, measure' – but ensure that what you are measuring is meaningful from a management perspective – and against a constant baseline – rather than redundant technical information provided by such theoretical devices such as function point counting.

I would not want to give the impression that the Project Manager's progress report is nothing but a table of numerical analyses. Far from it. Interpretation will inevitably require elucidation into a language that should be reasonably understood by all. Narrative to outline issues or expand on trends shown will be essential, with the data being used as evidence to support the analysis. Again, this offers up another trap for the unwary.

Let us assume that the last four weeks have shown an increasing trend in terms of the number of issues that have been logged and remain outstanding. For the Project Manager to simply make this statement in the fashion, 'Here is a problem; and here is another problem' is not enough. You might well get a bronze star from recognising the problem, but you will have a better chance of getting a silver one if you propose a solution at the same time. Gold star? The problem never arises on the first place!

So, let us turn our attention once again to answering the question 'where are we?'. This can be further sub-divided into any number of component questions; here we will tackle four:

? How de we 'read' progress?
? How should we track activities?
? When do we act?
? When and how do we update the project plan?

Reading Progress

The normal sequence of events on most well-managed projects is that weekly data relating to time spent and tasks completed is fed into the project planning tool and an updated view of the project is thus derived. Bars change shape or colour depending on the data entered and, with the exception of some subtle differences, the picture usually appears to remain pretty much as it was. Fair assessment?

Under these circumstances, there is no way that Project Managers can really read progress. Indeed, even if they spend hours pouring over the new Gantt chart they have produced, the sum of their findings might be that this or that task is late, and that this or that task will need more resource. Important of course, and vital when it comes to updating the plan, but insufficient to give an overall picture of health. In this scenario, when the Project Manager is faced with subtle changes week in, week out, it is all too easy for the project to drift from his control. Compare the plan after week twelve with that from week six and you might be in for a bit of a shock!

This is where the use of trend analysis can help. After all, it is quite simple to define what would be regarded as an ideal scenario – particularly at the end of the project: all activities complete; no spend over budget; no outstanding issues; all risks pacified; all changes dealt with. Not much chance of that, is there? But the Project Manager can define what would be acceptable – or 'normal' – within parameters, i.e. the profile within which he is comforta control and management. Consider the following as an exan. 20 week project:

Measure	Week 5	Week 10	Week 15	Week 2
Percentage of outstanding milestones which are late	< 15%	< 15%	< 10%	0
Expected work days effort required (% to estimate)	±7%	±10%	±7%	±5% *
Expected budget required (% to estimate)	±7%	±10%	±7%	±5% *
Risk assessment score	< 45%	< 35%	< 25%	< 15%
Number of outstanding issues	< 8	< 10	< 4	0

Note: * Otherwise known as contingency

This is of course, merely an illustrative example, but it does show how a Project Manager can (a) define his expectations for the project, and (b) 'read' where he is by comparing reality to this model.

Against such a Project Performance Profile, the Project Manager can easily identify significant divergence. Indeed, defining such a profile at the outset of the project – and the measures that make it up – can assist the manager in both knowing what to measure and knowing what to report.

More traditional methods – which attempt to use every statistic under the sun – can be no better than confusing. Consider the analysis below: do you have any idea from this how well the project is going?

Measure	Est.	Now	Measure	Est.	Now
Number of Tasks Started	27	24	Number of Issues Open	N/A	19
Number of Tasks Completed	14	16	Number of Issues Closed	N/A	4
Effort on Completed Tasks	64	59	Percentage of Issues Closed	N/A	15
Effort on Outstanding Tasks	287	304	Number of Changes logged	N/A	9
Effort on All Tasks	351	363	Budget Estimate to-date	327k	285k
Number of Tasks in the plan	75	83	Final Budget Estimate	1270k	1250k

And so on … hopeless, isn't it?

Tracking activities

The assessment above begs the question, 'how do we track activities?'

Traditionally this has been by recording time spent to the lowest possible level, which in turn leads to the kind of analysis dismissed above. Such an approach is based on a fundamental belief that management at the lowest level is necessary in order to enable control. Today's IT project – moving as it does in a much more dynamic and fast-paced environment – cannot afford to be bogged down in this kind of morass. With this in mind, project plans should, as we have suggested, be milestone- or deliverable-driven. Does it matter, for example, whether it takes six or sixty discretely planned activities to produce a single deliverable? Of course not! What matters is that the deliverable is produced to time and budget. It may be necessary to plan at a particular level to define accurately timescale and budgets for each milestone or deliverable (and these should be synonymous, remember) but the truest measure of progress – and the most manageable – has to be at the milestone level.

Indeed, there is an argument to suggest that, even if the project plan does define significant levels of detail within each deliverable, you should only record data at the milestone level; the assumption being that this reduces administration overhead and that such aggregation ultimately leads to the same results (from a reporting data perspective). This approach only works, however, if there are sufficient milestones within the plan, and that these occur frequently, i.e. there isn't a gap of two months between them.

This last statement provides a guide as to the level to which the Project Manager should track. Logically, you will only know if you are making progress if something does – or does not – happen. Therefore, at whatever level you track activities – or milestones – your plan should be driven by the need to regularly identify when things have or have not occurred. If milestones are two months apart (even though they should not be and this might suggest there are problems with your planning method) track at the activity level, **because these tasks represent things that should have happened.** If your milestones are set to occur on a weekly basis – or even more frequently – then track at the milestone-level, **because these represent things that should have been delivered.**

Taking action

Asking the question 'when do we act?' may seem a little vacuous in that the Project Manager should be continually working away at the successful implementation of his project. Taking this as read, the question is perhaps more valid if rephrased to be 'what leads the Project Manager to take significant action on the project with respect to the plan or the project's overall goals and objectives?' In other words, when do we know that things are beginning to go pear-shaped?

We have already provided a possible answer to this question in our discussion on reading progress. If the Project Manager embarks on his way with a Project Performance Profile in his mind, then these concrete measurables can act as trigger points. Indeed, along with statements relating to project constraints and assumptions, there is an argument for including the Project Performance Profile in any Initiation Report both to demonstrate an understanding of the task ahead, and also to clearly define triggers for action.

Contrary to first impressions perhaps, it is relatively easy to define key initiators for the Project Manager to step outside of his 'overview' management role and into 'resolution mode'. For example:

- to resolve a specific issue
- to address a specific risk
- to manage uncontrolled change
- when quality standards are compromised
- as a result of a negative audit
- to respond to situations where the project slips 'out of bounds', beyond the performance profile, e.g. is progressing towards being late, over-budget, beyond scope, and so on.

In many of the instances driven by the above criteria, the Project Manager will need to rein in maverick elements by making alterations to the project plan, i.e. thereby reassuming control.

Updating the plan

There is nothing particularly magical about the ability to change a project plan. Indeed, when you break it down to its constituent parts, the scope for change is – at its lowest level – somewhat limited. Given that the plan represents a combination of tasks and resources, we might summarise our options as follows:

- add or delete tasks
- change estimates of resource requirements on a task
- add or delete resources
- change resource availability profiles
- amend resource assignments.

I exclude budget explicitly here as almost any combination of the above will have budgetary implications, and thus the argument must be that any changes to the budget will be derived by – and will need to be driven by – changes to the plan. After all, how do you know how much more money you might need unless you define what it is additionally that you need to do?

The suggestion that it is relatively straightforward to update a project plan will seem like heresy to many, particularly those whose raison d'être is to spend six hours a week endeavouring to mirror reality in a Gantt chart. If you need to change the plan – because of scope creep, for example – then do so in accordance with the process and method that was used to draw it up, not on an ad-hoc basis or because it is Monday morning.

I did say, if you need to change the plan. For the old school of Project Manager, the plan would be changed as a matter of course every week, most commonly bombarded by changes to resource assignments and tweaking with timescale and effort estimates. The danger with this kind of approach is that you lose the continuity needed to make any trend analysis meaningful. Thirty changes to the plan one week; what effect does that have on the interpretation of next week's 'numbers' in relation to this week's?

So – and this will set alarm bells ringing in some quarters – endeavour not to change the plan as a matter of course. If a task is late and you need to allow more effort against it, do so – but do not change the plan to cater for this, but utilise contingency. The danger if you do change the plan too regularly, is that although your project appears to be moving closer and closer to estimates of effort and timescale at the micro level, it is in fact out of control, moving further and further away from its original course. Outside of the need to cater for additional tasks driven by a well-managed change management process (the re-assignment of contingency – see later), alterations to the plan should, in my view, be significant moments which are effectively re-plans – and re-plans driven by significant divergence from the original course (beyond the performance profile perhaps, or as a result of changing scope) when a new plan requires sponsor sign-off and a subsequent redefinition of the baseline.

Regular and unjustified changes to the plan by the Project Manager represent his own not-insignificant contribution to the uncontrolled.

This discussion of tracking and making alterations to the plan brings us back to the issue of change management and how the Project Manager should tackle it. Before we can consider the practice and process of change management however, we need to identify exactly what constitutes change.

From a purist perspective, any deviation from the project plan represents change. Based on the path that has been set out with the aim of achieving the goals that have been set, any movement away is – by definition – change. Furthermore, it is uncontrolled change in that it must also logically follow that some remedial action will be required to reassume control. In the real world of IT project management, to take such a stance would be ludicrous as the Project Manager would be dealing with change on a daily if not hourly basis. In many respects, those who insist on the weekly massaging of the project plan fall into this school of thinking.

Plainly, to take this approach is ludicrous. Equally, the opposite extreme – to allow the project to meander until it reaches its natural conclusion – while it may satisfy some mystical Eastern philosophy, is also a non-starter. The key, therefore, is to recognise what constitutes meaningful change; and by change we broadly mean advent of the unexpected – and therefore initially uncontrolled – which will have a significant impact on the project. Bearing in mind that it is natural for things to be fluid, we need to identify what might change, and where that change becomes significant, i.e. where the impact of the change exceeds tolerances catered for within the project's current contingency budget and/or where re-drafting of the project plan becomes a distinct possibility.

Going back to the basic elements of the project is useful here:

What might change	What might be seen as significant impact
Project goals and objectives; 'scope creep'	• Additional tasks, effort and cost to the project which exceed contingency tolerances • Extension of projected end-date • Change of business goals
Resource changes	• Loss or unavailability of key resources
Effort estimates	• Evidence that estimates for a number of key tasks are significantly low
Late delivery	• Increasing numbers of milestones not being hit
Running beyond budget	• Spend to-date running well above that projected
Increasing risks and issues	• Numbers of open items is increasing without check

Of course, it is impossible to give an absolute value to these. A 5% overspend on one project may be perfectly allowable, whilst on another it would spell disaster. Similarly losing two people from a team of 30 might represent a hiccup, but from a team of five ...?

Having identified a Project Performance Profile in advance helps the Project Manager to quantify 'significance' ahead of the game; it enables him to define his levels of tolerance at 5% or 10% or 15% as appropriate. It also allows him to provide the project sponsor with an early warning mechanism as trends push certain measures towards the red zone. Using such a schema, there can be no ambiguity; subjective interpretation – particularly of those outside project management – can be dismissed, given that solid facts exist to support any conclusions drawn.

In as much as a mechanism is needed for logging and tracking risks and issues then, something similar is required for changes; though the key here is not closure in the sense that risks or issues are 'closed', but closure in the sense that the change is being managed and moved into an environment where it is 'controlled'. A change management programme should therefore record at least the following:

● some kind of reference number
● title and description

- priority
- date entry was raised and the person who initiated the change
- external reference, e.g. risk or issue reference which led to the change being requested
- status, i.e. open (i.e. unaddressed), closed (i.e. incorporated into the project plan), rejected (i.e. change will not be made)
- any action required and the person charged with taking that action (it might not be as simple as adding a task to the plan)
- impact of incorporating the change: this should be in concrete terms; effort, time and/or cost
- sign-off authority
- date the change is signed off or rejected.

At the micro-level, this kind of log will provide an appropriate mechanism for keeping track of those potential additions to and deviations from the original plan. Like risks and issues, the log will need regular management, with the frequency of this process – which must include business users if the project is a business project – set in scale with the project: a two-year project, perhaps fortnightly; a two-week project, perhaps daily.

So you now have your change management process in place, sitting nicely alongside those for risks and issues; you have defined the performance profile in advance, so all those associated with the project know where your trigger limits are set. More importantly perhaps, having incorporated a degree of contingency into your original plan – see how import this is now?! – you are able to turn uncontrolled change requests into controlled elements within the plan without compromising the end-date or the budget. Sounds okay, doesn't it? But only if you know how to manage contingency.

In Section Four, we considered ways not only of calculating contingency needed on a project, but also how it might be incorporated. Perhaps the most straightforward approach is to define contingency as a single task at the very end of the project, with the final delivery date given as being the end of that contingency task, not the beginning of it. This method provides the most straightforward means of managing contingency in association with a change management programme. Let us consider an example.

We have a project that we have calculated will run for 20 weeks, utilising five people on a full-time basis. Including non-productive activities – and more of these soon! – this aggregates to 500 work days of effort. We have also calculated that we need 10% contingency, i.e. 50 work days, or 2 elapsed weeks based on the team of five. Four weeks into the plan, three changes have arisen which need to be incorporated. These are as follows:

		R e s o u r c e s				
Change	**A**	**B**	**C**	**D**	**E**	**Total**
1	1 day					1 day
2		1 day		3 days		4 days
3			1 day	1 day	2 days	4 days

These changes total 9 days effort; easily within the 50 work days allocated. If we were utilising a tool such as Microsoft Project, a task could be added for each of these three changes, with the resource allocations against the 'blanket' contingency task reduced by the amounts shown, i.e. resource A from 10 to 9 days, and so forth. On this basis, we have turned our uncontrolled requests into managed changes, and catered for them in the plan without compromising the end date (unless there are severe dependencies or elapsed time considerations – such as hardware lead times – which should trigger a review anyway).

Now let us consider two further tasks. Change 4 requires 5 days from both resources B and C, and change 5 requires 8 days from resource D. The total contingency now consumed by the changes is 27 days. As this is still well within our 50 days allowance, we have no issues, right?

Wrong! Of these 27 days, 12 are now required from resource D. Having allowed only 10 from each resource this means that either (a) some of D's existing workload needs to be reallocated, or (b) we have a warning that we are likely to miss the end date – D has become a critical resource. Having established contingency, knowing how to handle it is a key aspect of the Project Manager's role – assuming that situations like this have been recognised in the first instance.

If we assume that the workload for changes could be evenly spread across all five resources, when do we need to consider re-planning?

When we break the 50 day allowance? Hardly. But where is the trigger? Can it be an absolute number? Would hitting 40 days do it?

I have to say not. There is a significant difference between using 40 days contingency by the end of week three compared to the end of week nineteen. Again, think about tolerances and triggers in advance, and recognise where issues are likely to arise before they do. Again using our example above, consider where our trigger points might be in terms of allocated/used contingency:

Week	1	2	3	4	5	6	7	8	9	10
Trigger	10	13	16	19	22	24	26	28	30	32

Week	11	12	13	14	15	16	17	18	19	20
Trigger	33	34	35	36	38	40	42	45	48	50

Of course you might want to be a little more considered than this, basing your assessment on where you are in the project at any one time – but you get the message.

For some projects, of course, the critical element might be money rather than time. Again, the same kind of process applies – both in terms of drawing off the contingency and in identifying trigger points in advance. Indeed, if you think of contingency as savings set aside for a rainy day, you will get the idea here. All you need to do is hope there is no prolonged deluge!

People management

There are undoubtedly myriad issues faced by the Project Manager with respect to the management of human resources throughout the duration of the project. One arises not from negative forces, but from the very positive ambition to contribute as significantly as possible – yet from a basis of naïve ignorance or lack of experience. We discussed earlier the relationship between estimates and reality, and the unmistakable conclusion that an estimate can only ever be an average. Enthusiasm therefore – sometimes coupled with a lack of professional hardening – can often lead the project in the exact opposite direction to that intended.

How often does, 'I can do that in three days!' lead to a task that takes in excess of a week? How many times do development and testing estimates assume that the number of errors will be minuscule or the rework time is negligible? Can this be avoided? Often not. This is particularly true when the Project Manager is working with people who are not previously known to them. 'Three days' has to be taken at face value.

Some simple techniques can contribute to putting quality into the estimating process and rein back unbridled enthusiasm. If time allows – and if you can persuade people not to be too precious about their estimates – ask for a second opinion from other members of the team; vet those estimates given where, without any relevant experience of your own to act as a guide, you have no means of sanity checking yourself. An example would be where the project involved a development tool unknown to the Project Manager. Exactly how long does it take to build a fully functioning HTML web page? If you do not know, ask two people to estimate for the same thing.

Avoidance of the over-ambitious may not be achievable. Under these circumstances, empirical evidence can assist. If, for example, someone had estimated five tasks to take twenty days and they have actually taken thirty, consider increasing other estimates that person has given by an appropriate factor; in this case 50%. (Similarly, you can make the adjustment the other way of course – most useful!) If you suspect from the outset that this situation might occur and thus negatively impact the project, then ensure you consider this at initiation time when calculating contingency.

Someone attempting to give you the answer you want to hear can generate a similar effect. If, for example, they know a task really needs to be complete in a week, then 'five days' may be the most obvious answer – even if it is wrong. Sanity checking and pro-active adjustment are the Project Manager's only tools in this circumstance.

Instilling the need for realism when asking for estimates is essential – the success of the whole project may well be dependent on the quality of the estimates after all. Encouraging honest appraisal in difficult circumstances is also a key attribute for the Project Manager: 'I know I'd like it done in a week, but how long will it really take? I'll worry about the knock-on effect ...'

Managing this particular issue is only one of a number of supervisory tricks the Project Manager needs to rely on. As is widely recognised, this type of management is vastly different from the exercise of control that might have elevated the manager to his lofty position in the first place, i.e. the experience of managing technology. Maintaining control and morale is critical to success, and while the two may appear to clash at first, this is not the case. A team who feels they are working in a controlled, well-managed and balanced or harmonious environment will undoubtedly enjoy better morale than those who do not.

Tackling the psychology of people management is a subject for other books, but noting the key pointers cannot go amiss. Recognise the importance of internal communication. As much as possible, communicate within the team environment with respect to issues and decisions which might affect the whole. This can be done not only through full team meetings, but also through a management sub-team, with messages cascaded down through the team or department hierarchy. Such an approach offers a number of critical advantages to the Project Manager.

✔ It ensures all have the same view and understanding.
✔ It fosters a sense of collective ownership.
✔ It will generate buy-in.
✔ It aids in team building.
✔ It prevents a sense of disenfranchisement.
✔ It might just provide some feedback which is critical to project success.

Undertaking such a commitment – and it is a commitment on the part of the Project Manager, not the team – can sometimes be difficult or time consuming; but the end result should repay multi-fold.

Non-productive time
One area in which this approach can be seen to bear fruit in a tangible way is in the reduction in non-productive time. But what is non-productive time? And how do we manage it?

On virtually any project of reasonable scale – or on any accumulation of projects over a period of time – non-productive time will nearly always equate to around 15%, give or take a little. Why so confident? Well, first consider what non-productive time is. A definition: 'effort expended which contributes nothing towards a project-related deliverable.' Thus:

- holidays
- sickness
- administration
- general training.

Management can also be added to this list when referring to high-level, departmental management rather than specific project management. Holidays will take 20 days from a maximum working potential of around 250. General admin – which includes filling in the timesheets that gives the Project Manager this information! – around another 6 to 12, depending on the processes in place. General training might average out to 5 days per person. Not all people will be sick, but the average across the team might be 3 or 4 days. This gives us between 34 to 41 days non-productive time; or an average of 37.5 – 15% of the total.

These numbers are not artificial. Years of personal experience plus anecdotal input from other Project Managers confirm that 15% is the right mark at which to aim – this means it needs to be recognised in the project plan up-front (see Section Four). Given such a guideline, it becomes easy to recognise where there might be issues:

- **Individuals who regularly record over 20%** of non-productive time. More than a day a week! Are they being lazy or do they simply not understand the system, i.e. the use of the 'admin' bucket code for all the time they can't recall how to allocate

- **Individuals who regularly record less than 5%.** Are they just trying to impress, or perhaps they are not carrying out the admin-related tasks they should be.

- **Teams who regularly record in excess of say 17% or 18%.** This suggests that there may be significant issues with the management of the project or department.

Note: remember that non-productive time is seasonal; there will be more in summer!

So, being in a position to measure and monitor, the Project Manager can identify both that there is an issue and, hopefully, what the source is. This allows him to focus on a solution. Remember again, that if the plan allows for 15% overhead and you are incurring more, then the project will almost certainly be slipping behind schedule – and you might not realise it.

One further thought in this area. It should be recognised that if the project is multi-site or multi-national, then for some people within the team, non-productive time may well be higher. This can come about through an increase in things like travel, management meetings or general administration. There are additional issues in such an environment too.

The communication we have just spoken about becomes critical as geography will almost inevitable create 'local' teams which will develop their own ethos and philosophy, particularly in satellite locations. Standardisation of process and communication becomes even more important therefore, as the Project Manager will want to be as sure as he can be that, when considering metrics from each location, he is actually comparing apples with apples rather than trying to make sense of a fruit cocktail.

Maintaining a focal point with respect to contact between locations can be useful too, with a team made up of a single individual from each location forming a management group in its own right, feeding in issues and ideas from the periphery which are more likely than not to be invisible from the centre.

Having said all of this, the Project Manager needs to be wary of over-control; of attempting to put so much 'management' in place that the project could be compromised. Again, careful monitoring of non-productive time can be incredibly useful – as will be the barometer provided by the experienced Project Manager's 'nose' – you can usually smell when something is bad!

The people problem

There is a sad truism – 'a project is only as good as its people'. Sad? Because it is often trotted out by senior management, but never believed in – and because this is a trap the Project Manager can fall into only too easily. So two simple questions: 'how do you get good people?' and 'how do you keep them once you've got them?'

In order to get good resources the Project Manager working in an IT environment at the beginning of the twenty-first century needs to recognise two key factors: firstly, that he is almost certainly operating in a sellers market; and secondly, that when it comes to recruiting staff, he needs to be a good salesman. This is difficult for many, so here are four simple tips:

Believe in the Project. You need to believe in the product you are selling – your project – that it will work, and that it will deliver. People need to feel their manager is committed; if he isn't, why should they be?

Believe in the Strategy. You should be able to articulate the strategy within which your project fits, and provide a reference framework for it. People like to see the 'Big Picture'.

Be enthusiastic about the future. The strategy-project combination should point to a future that is positive and full of opportunity. People like to know what's next.

Be clear about where they fit in. Have a firm view on the role and responsibility on offer, what the individual will be expected to contribute to the overall goal, and which of his or her skills are most attractive. People need to feel wanted and that they can bring something to the party; don't give them the impression that they are just another body.

If you can convince people of these four elements, then they may already be hooked by the time it comes to discuss money!

Of course, once you have the right people, there comes the problem of keeping them. If all goes according to plan – and everyone can still actually see and justifiably believe in those things outlined above – then you are more than half way towards maintaining a stable and happy workforce. Indeed, one of the advantages of any annual appraisal system (viewed by the majority as a pain!) is that it gives the Project Manager a chance to sell an updated version of the future to his team. If you treat part of the appraisal as a selling job, then wage negotiations can be easier too!

Inevitably, someone will want to leave – but before this happens, it is worth while the Project Manager assessing the cost of not keeping him or her, rather than the cost of replacement. The difference? The cost of replacement is often seen as the equation:

Salary of new person – salary of old person
Or ... £38,000 – £35,000 – therefore £3,000

Not too bad, eh? Assuming an internal work day rate of £400, what about the (opportunity) cost of not keeping them:

Period of demotivation/wind down:	75 % efficiency over 20 days	£2,000
Management time for recruitment	Recruitment agency liaison – 2 days	£800
	Interviewing – 4 days	£1,600
Gap between leaver and starter	20 days (for example)	£8,000
Period of inefficiency for new starter	75% efficiency over 40 days	£4,000
Additional training requirement	5 days	£2,000
	Cost of Course	£1,400

Illustrative, I know, but suddenly our £3,000 cost has been increased by another £16,800 in terms of 'opportunity cost'. So when someone you don't want to lose tells you that they are leaving because they have been offered an additional £4,000 elsewhere, think twice before just letting them go.

Money may not be the issue, of course. If there are problems with team dynamics and personalities, then it may be financially beneficial to incur the kind of costs outlined above. No amount of money will help under these circumstances, nor if the individual has simply stopped believing in what you are selling. But if money is the crux of the matter – and if your hands are tied in terms of increasing salary or other financial incentives such as bonuses – then try other forms of tie-in; suggest promotion, or a new role. Basically, see if you can realistically and honestly modify your sales pitch to win them back.

People will leave; it is inevitable. The Project Manager needs to be clear about what can happen at the time of a resignation.

✘ A negative message goes out to the team, i.e. something's wrong, or the grass is greener elsewhere.

✘ Productivity may be impacted across the board.

✖ Other people may start asking questions and look elsewhere.

Don't get nervous – this will only exacerbate the problem. What you are actually facing is a change management issue; and certainly this may be true as far as the project and its plan is concerned. If the individual who is going is expendable – perhaps he or she is not that productive or is generally not well regarded by peers – then the opposite of the three things identified above might actually occur! So losing people can be good – be prepared to let the expendable go!

For key people you know you would not want to lose, prepare in advance at least the notion of a succession plan. Always have a view on who could step up should someone critical leave. And always try to recruit a replacement internally if at all possible. Why?

Internal Promotion	External Appointment
• Positive message about growing from within	• Gives message that current resources aren't good enough
• Will allow you to re-sell to someone already on board, thereby gaining a significant period of fresh buy-in	• May shorten future buy-in period for many on the project
• Acts as stimulus to others: they are well-regarded and there will be opportunities	• May serve to inflate salary demands across the board (assuming new person is more expensive)
• Recruiting at the bottom to back-fill is positive message for all	• Can start an unfortunate spiral
• Likely to have least impact on overall productivity	• Is the more expensive option
• Can stop a trickle from becoming a flood	

Laying mines

Before we leave this section of the book behind and embark on our final consideration – elements of project management execution – we need to conclude with a short consideration on three aspects relating to IT projects which can scupper the best laid of plans: maintenance; the PC epidemic; over-documentation.

The maintenance spiral

We have considered elsewhere the implications of implementing package solutions to meet the functional needs of the business. The theory of an 'out of the box' solution is fine – until the first modification is made, that is. One might argue that we are merely in change management mode at this point, and that we have our techniques and tools for managing these. Indeed, and why should making amendments to bought packages present any additional problems? Of course they don't – not, that is, until the supplier brings out a new version of the software.

The 'impossibility of vanilla' was something we considered in Part Four, and I raise it again here to re-emphasise how success – in the delivery of a project – can lead to failure later, when the cost of maintenance becomes suddenly prohibitive or restrictive. As part of solution design, always consider options for additional functionality rather than simply amending your virgin software. Try the constant interface approach or the incorporation of discrete modules, rather than accepting the change. And at the end of the project, recognise closure not as the end of a project, but the beginning of the transition to the next.

Personal computers

When PCs arrived in the business world, IT professionals were suddenly presented with a tool which allowed them to break free of the old 'green on black' application, and give users a more dynamic, attractive and intuitive interface. How things have moved on! Unfortunately, however, we have now reached the situation where most users actually regard the PC that sits on their desk as 'belonging' to them. After all, it has their favourite screensaver and wallpaper, the icons have been customised to meet their favourite theme and layout, and all of the productivity software applications – such as Word and Excel – have customised toolbars designed for their own way of working.

The PC is a nightmare to maintain for the IT function, and reining them in can prove to be a task too far for many. In addition to needing control – for the installation and support of corporate business software, for example – the IT manager also finds himself with an ever increasing demand on his budget as gradually more and more power is required as more and more functionality is on offer. In the majority of instances, this scenario will be in situ for the Project Manager, and often these issues will not fall within his remit. However, if the Project Manager is ever fortunate enough to be in a 'green field' situation, then he should consider his options, both at strategy definition (if he has the chance) and at application design. Some tips:

✓ Review what is really needed by the end user – individual customised functionality, or slick interface to a common application?

✓ Consider the possibility of using thin clients or network PCs with all application software resident on a common server architecture.

✓ Investigate options which allow some local variation but which enforce, from the centre, an automated routine to keep the machines 'clean'.

These approaches may not be popular initially, but they will without doubt save the project or department money, both in terms of support as well as helping to reduce the frequency with which equipment needs replacing.

Over-documentation

Akin to the inexperienced and over-enthusiastic estimator, very often Project Managers burden their projects – and their staff – with a commitment to deliver a Rolls Royce solution in terms of supporting documentation. Bound manuals with sparkly, laminated covers; reams of guide sheets or 'hints and tips'; page after page of elaborately illustrated case studies and tutorial material.

What a waste! The Project Manager needs to recognise that after a short period, users of a new system will no longer need paper documents to support them because they will simply know how to use the new application. Training is the key issue to resolve, not documentation.

So ask some questions:

? What is really needed – and why is it needed? How can it be justified?

? What is the life-span of the documentation to be produced? If less than three months, it must be in question.

? Who is going to produce it? What will be the impact on the project? Is it planned?

? What kind of quality is needed? And what is the best mechanism for delivery?

Perhaps the most useful clue is to ask some business users what they wished they had – either now or in the past – from the last new system that was implemented and affected them. You might be surprised by the answer!

6

Execution

A Dying Skill

Whilst many projects will fail through poorly defined scope, an inability to manage change, unacceptable risks and so forth, a few will never deliver to their full potential as a result of a structural weakness which exposes a skill gap. In our modern development environment with its ever more sophisticated computer-aided engineering software, one skill has become a rare commodity; that of the analyst. Consider the historical passage thus far:

- Programmers and analysts were recognised as separate skills in the days of 2nd and 3rd generation development languages (such as COBOL).

- The advent of the personal computer gave rise to new tools, initially with BASIC.

- As more power became transferred to the desktop – and as 'look and feel' become paramount – the 'importance of function' become overshadowed by the 'appearance of function'.

- A new breed of developer was born – the analyst programmer or systems engineer – where the two roles were merged and became blurred.

- Development tools became even more sophisticated, apparently removing the need for much of the 'analyst' portion in the role; more and more the tool did the work.

- True analytical skills become dinosaur-like.

Perhaps a generalisation – but consider what we typically no longer do in application development projects. Key for me are the facts that (a) requirements are seldom defined by a trained analyst, (b) functional test models are rarely developed, and (c) 'programs' go straight from the developer's keyboard to the user's desk.

Evidently, we need to move with the technological times, and I am not advocating a return to the traditional 'life cycle' of a project, but consider what modern development tools cannot do – and remember that developers are now trained to use the functionality provided by the tools, not defining what they are really doing from a business perspective.

How much of these kinds of skills were missing from your last development project?

- Asking questions of the business in terms of the function they required – or was it simply a matter of translating what was **thought** to be required into code?

- Who thinks sideways when a user asks for 'X'?
  Who says 'If you have 'X', what happens when this event occurs?' or 'Okay, you say you want 'X', but wouldn't 'Y' be better?' Software tools do not do this.

- Where is the 'What if?' analysis carried out?
  'What if A is greater than B?'
  'What if the user doesn't press the Enter key now?'
  'What if there's a new product line?'
  'What if…?'

- Who adds the value of their experience? For the development tool, the beginning of every project is the same as the last, which means there is no guarantee that the same mistakes – from the point of view of business function – will not be made again.

On development projects designed to deliver business function – aren't they all? – good analytical skills are a must. In addition to addressing all the issues above, the analyst is a key deliverer of quality; not only will the function delivered be more robust and a tighter fit to the business, it will also be of a higher quality – particularly if the analyst tests the software before handing it over to the user.

So a plea for the analyst. If your project is about delivering business function, have at least two. Call them analysts, make sure they are analysts, and give them true analyst roles. It may take a little longer to deliver your project, but it will be closer to what's really needed (remember often the users do not know what they want and need to be challenged) and it is more likely to work first time.

Getting a quality product live

As we suggested above, absence of a recognised and dedicated Analyst can have a negative impact on an application delivery from a quality perspective. In other types of project too, the lack of what might be termed a 'functional consultant' can lead to similar disappointments. One generic element in all of this is the approach to testing, with business application delivery being the arena where this impact is most likely to be felt.

Traditional development life cycles defined fairly prescriptive stages for testing and those who would ideally be involved. Consider the table below to see how the modern development environment has affected this schema:

	Traditional	Modern
Unit testing	Planned and executed by programmer	Rarely formally planned, executed by developer
Integration testing	Planned by analyst, executed with programmer	Step rarely applicable
System testing	Planned by analysts, executed by entire team	Rarely formally planned, executed by development team
Acceptance testing	Planned by users & analysts, executed by users	Rarely planned, executed by user community

Whilst not true in all cases, as a generic example it can immediately be seen how – through both lack of analytical skills and abdication of responsibility to the development tools themselves – it is inevitable that the quality of the end product, from a functional perspective if nothing else, is being compromised.

Of particular concern in this model is how the responsibility for testing is increasingly placed upon the end user who may actually be testing something that was only vaguely conceived in the first instance. Additionally, these are people who not only lack the intimate knowledge of systems development which means that they may not know how to test, but they are also unlikely to be that committed to such a process, the assumption being that by the time they get their hands on any application it should be 'finished' and work first time. This situation is not just down to any failing of the IT community. Very often the pressure from the business to deliver in ever shorter timeframes leads to the cutting of corners – and this must mean that testing will suffer.

Again using an outline similar to that above, let us consider the kinds of benefits and deficits associated with testing programmes. We will assume that the program in question requires 20 logical functional processes to be performed, and – after coding – contains a number of errors:

		Traditional			Modern		
		Effort	Functions	Errors	Effort	Functions	Errors
1	Requirement definition	20	18	0	10	14	0
2	Development	50	16	40	30	12	20
3	Unit testing	10	17	8	5	13	12
4	System/integration testing	10	18	4	0	13	12
5	Acceptance testing	5	19	2	3	16	6
	Totals	**95**			**48**		

Note: By 'Functions' in the table above, I mean those functions that have been defined, developed, tested and accepted in a satisfactory manner (stages 1, 2, 4 and 5).

In this example, we can see how a traditional approach to both design and testing would have taken nearly twice as long to pass into a 'live' environment. However, 95% of the function actually required would have been delivered and the system would contain only 2 errors (as opposed to 20% of the functionality required being missing, and there being 6 errors in the live system). These numbers can be extrapolated to take into consideration rework in the live environment, re-testing etc.

From the Project Manager's perspective, he needs to understand at the commencement of the project – i.e. at the planning stage – what approach he is going to take to testing. This will most likely be dictated by any imposed timescales and/or the absence of resources. There are clearly two ends to this particular spectrum, and the one towards which the Project Manager will gravitate should ultimately be driven by the nature of the business application – i.e. is it financial? – and its criticality to the business.

Wherever the Project Manager places his strategy along the testing spectrum, one of the most crucial issues he is likely to face is in arranging and completing user acceptance testing. There are a number of key factors: getting commitment to business resources; defining an appropriately rigorous test plan; and ensuring satisfactory execution. Without doubt, this is something that needs to be sold by the Project Manager – which is a little ironic considering the project is almost certainly there for the benefit of the business.

As indicated earlier in this book, very often the issue is one of perceived ownership too: it's an IT project, and therefore why should the business need to get involved?

If the Project Manager has established business champions for the project and has an enthusiastic sponsor, then half the battle may already be won. However, never under-estimate the amount of effort – and time – required to ensure that user testing executes in a satisfactory manner its responsibility towards an overall quality check. With this in mind, the Project Manager needs to ensure that key business users are explicitly engaged at this stage. Someone from the IT team will need to sit down with them and assist in the drawing up of the users' test plan – possibly undertaking to generate the test data themselves. They will then need to work with the users and assist in the execution of the tests. Finally they will need to document and co-ordinate any re-work and re-testing.

Such an approach may sound suspiciously like systems or integration testing, and in many respects it is; however it may be the only way to ensure users exercise their testing responsibility towards the project. Providing a test environment and expecting the business community to just 'get on with it' is a luxury that only a few organisations – with a forward thinking user base – can afford. So, if user acceptance is a requirement for productionisation – as it should be – then say so at the commencement of the project, but be prepared to help users get there. If a concrete justification is needed, work up some numbers based on the rough example above; it's not just quality now, it's the maintenance overhead later on.

Similar issues – those of user resource and commitment – are also often associated with application training, particularly when the degree of effort required or depth of understanding to be imparted is considerable. In much the same way as user testing needs to be planned, so the Project Manager faces a similar task with training; and in many respects – such as leaving the organisation of such a key activity until the last minute – the approach taken is unfortunately similar. As with the testing example given above, it is entirely feasible to make out a reasonably concrete case for not only putting the right degree of training in place, but also ensuring all users attend their appropriate session(s). For example, consider the impact on initial support overhead measured in estimated hours per user per month:

Level of Testing	50% of Users	75% of Users	100% of Users
Low / Perfunctory	10 hours	8 hours	4 hours
Medium / Adequate	6 hours	4 hours	2 hours
High / Comprehensive	4 hours	2 hours	1 hour

Hardly scientific – but multiply the estimates by the number of users and then calculate the cost equivalent based on a work day rate for IT support staff ...

There are other issues particular to end-user training that the wise Project Manager will endeavour not only to assess at an early stage, but also to schedule in to his project plan:

- Will training be carried out by internal or external staff? Cost vs. resource impact issue.

- Will all users be trained, or will a 'Train the Trainer' approach be taken? Certainty over consistency of message vs. cost and resource implications.

- Should IT staff or users deliver the training? Business-based – which is better but is likely to take longer to prepare fully –

vs. IT-based – which may be 'quicker' but lack the business perspective.

- When should the training be delivered? Too early and there may be a gap between completion and 'go live'; too late, and not all users may be trained before 'go live'.

Whichever approach is taken – and this will be driven by the individual project, its implementation circumstances, the users themselves, and most likely, politics – one approach often overlooked is the actual system 'launch'.

More often than not, application systems slide into production as ships slide down the slip-way, their bows making barely a splash. Okay, they may bobble about a little at first, but this is hardly a big event. Consider making more of productionisation; launch the ship side-on, if you will. This will ensure a bigger splash and an energetic launch will help the project team and the users recognise and mark the transition from old to new. It will also help to give the team a sense of achievement too. The ship will still bobble about of course – unfortunately this is inevitable!

User guides

We have already touched on the subject of documentation, and this goes hand-in-hand with training. The two should be complimentary, and leave no gaps between them once any system is in production. On this basis, the two should not – as is so often the case – be considered in isolation. For example, 100% user saturation in a quality training programme will significantly reduce the need for supporting documentation; possibly down to on-line help only. Superficial training will need to be backed up by better quality documentation. It really is a 'swings-and-roundabouts' scenario. Where do you, as Project Manager, want to spend your resource? And where can you effectively use either external agencies or the users themselves in the training vs. documentation equilibrium?

The bottom line probably lies in the generalisation that, 9 times out of 10, training is more effective than documentation.

So remember the questions we have already raised about documentation and apply these to user guides; for example, who really reads them?! And consider alternative options: perhaps a mouse mat with key facts about the system, such as navigation standards or coding rules; or a flip pad that sits beside the monitor with simple one-glance process guides for key elements within the system. Remember, user guides do not have to be made of paper and bound in 4-ring binders!

At the end of the day, there is a kind of balance which the Project Manager needs to strike in terms of the training-documentation-resource-timescale-cost-benefit equation which will be right for any one situation – though the result is unlikely to apply equally well to every project, as the key drivers (usually cost, timescale and/or user resource commitment/availability) are likely to vary. Potential impact of any constraint needs to be recognised as early as possible in order to plan for the post-implementation situation. For example:

Cost	Timescale	Users	Impact
OK	Limited	OK	Training is likely to be superficial for all or detailed for a few. There is likely to be insufficient time to produce detailed documentation. • Adopt a 'Train the Trainer' approach • Go for simple but effective essential support materials • Prepare for significant post-live support queries
Limited	OK	OK	All training and documentation will need to be handled in-house, without the scope for external specialised support • Go for reasonably detailed training - all users • Support with on-line help
OK	OK	Limited	There may be a need to provide significant material to assist with post-implementation queries. Some business-aspects may be omitted from the training if carried out by IT staff. • Adopt 'Train the Trainer' where feasible • Prepare quality supporting documentation (possibly outsourced) • Endeavour to ensure good knowledge of business function within IT support team • Prepare for significant post-live support queries

So, no easy answers – but then you haven't got this far without knowing that!

And finally, here a brief consideration of the impact of the relatively new phenomenon of 'validation'. Effectively testing by another name, validation relates to the fundamental proof that a product – be it hardware or software – actually performs the function for which it was designed and built, and in accordance with the specification given.

The most obvious example of the relevance of validation is in a manufacturing environment, for example, in a pharmaceutical situation where a machine used to form medicinal drugs needs to be proven to make the pills or capsules with exactly the right proportion of compound or ingredients. In other areas such as construction, absolute certainty that pre-formed steel joints perform in accordance with stress tolerance levels will be critical. In these instances it is not just the end products – the pills or joints – which need to be checked, but the very machinery which manufactures them.

Such in-depth testing is beginning to encroach into the IT arena. When a network hub is purchased, should it be 'validated' to ensure that it will perform exactly to specification? And what about package software, straight from a shrink-wrapped box? Or the brand new PC and its globally accepted operating system? How do we really know that they will work? Asking such questions can lead to technological paranoia. Once you have started down this slippery slope – and waved goodbye to conventional testing – exactly where does one stop?

Undoubtedly there will be projects where some critical elements, either hardware or software, will need some form of validation – usually because their ability to delivery 100% of what is expected on a consistent basis is critical to business success. If this is the case, then state the approach to validation at the very beginning of the project. Schedule in the tasks to accomplish any validation sign-off needed – taking care to remember that in many instances validation is likely to occur at the commencement of the project more so than at the end. Perhaps validation will be relevant on a small proportion of projects; but it is something to be aware of in the struggle to deliver a quality product.

The biggest picture of all

Imagine the scene: two years into your five-year strategic plan and the first three major projects have all gone like clockwork; the fourth is well under-way. Your business colleagues have been hanging bunting in your honour for the last six months, and there's even talk that one day – one day! – you might just make it to the board. Of course, the business is moving on too and flourishing, in part thanks to the splendidly consistent and reliable IT support it now enjoys. Happy? Content? Do your laurels have two round indentations in them through your recent predilection for sitting?

Perhaps some other questions.

? When was the last time you looked at your strategic plan?

? Are you making the assumption that, with three more years to run, you will not need to do anything with it for at least the next thirty months?

? Do you find yourself adopting the attitude that, now you've got it sorted, you don't really need a strategic plan after all?

? Is there now a belief that it was created more as a guide than anything else – something to persuade the business to give you an enlarged budget perhaps?

All too often, I suspect the answers to many of these questions will be 'yes', forgetting the fundamental point that completing a project is also delivery on an element of the strategy.

? When a task is completed, do we not check its impact on delivery of a milestone?

? When a milestone is hit, what is its impact on the project?

? Therefore, why, when a project is delivered, should we not return to its parent, the strategic plan for a similar review?

As has already been said in this book, the strategic plan should be a living document; something that outlines not only initial intentions, but also reflects both on attempts to deliver against those intentions and on any changes in the business which are bound to occur over time. Imagine, for example, a strategic plan at the beginning of the twenty-first century that did not address the impact of the internet on the business.

The secret must be to keep the strategy alive, not to consign it to the back of some cupboard never to be revisited.

How might we approach this? Firstly – and most simply – schedule a regular review of the strategic plan. Six monthly would seem to make sense (unless your business market is particularly volatile), and you should take a view as to whether the review is something undertaken by yourself or in concert with others; business operating factors may make this decision for you. If this review consists simply of refreshing your mind as to what was intended, then it's hardly worth bothering. The review needs to be a serious undertaking, perhaps with a whole day devoted to it – off-site if necessary.

Let us assume that in the six months since the plan was published and became 'live' the following scenario exists:

	In strategic plan		Actual events
1	Reconfiguration and upgrading of entire Head Office infrastructure: cost £300,000, due for completion at the end of month 4.		Work completed and new infrastructure commissioned towards the end of month 5. Final cost of project £340,000
2	Major ERP package implementation begun. Initial phase of requirements definition due for completion at the end of month 3, with invitation to tenders issued the following month. Package selection to be down to the last two short-listed candidates by the end of month 6; decision in month 7. Estimated spend to date, £42,000.		Requirements definition completed early in month 4. Invitations to tender issued according to plan. At the end of month 6, there are three short-listed candidates. Spend £39,000.
3	Roll-out of the UK's Human Resources administration systems to all international locations. Countries expected to be converted in the first six months, France and Germany: Spain and Switzerland in progress. Cost to date estimated at £97,000		France and Germany live, with Switzerland slightly ahead of schedule. Some problems in Spain with delivery expected to be delayed by about a month. (The business has now acquired new operations in Portugal, Greece and the Irish Republic.)
4	Redevelopment of three existing PC-based logistics systems into a new Java-driven application, allowing remote web-based access to non-UK sites. Planned to be live in month 5 at a cost of £27,000		Delivered to budget, though at the end of month 6.
5	Support and maintenance running at 35% of resource availability.		Support and maintenance estimated at 41%.
		6	Unplanned project to deliver an upgrade to the warehouse system begun in month 3. Due for completion in month 7 at a cost of £39,000.
		7	Two resignations in month 6 - one support person and the senior database administrator.

Let's be honest, not a bad curriculum vitae for the first six months of a new era! Overall progress has been good, things have been delivered, and the business should be feeling reasonably good about the service it is getting. Certainly one could be forgiven for feeling reasonably satisfied.

But let's have a look in detail – and from the strategic viewpoint ...

	Strategically	Strategic plan action
1	May just be budget over-spend. You may need to check things like amortisation assumptions. One question: has the one month slippage affected any work that was dependent on the new infrastructure?	• Review the strategic plan to take into account any knock-on effects. • Record actual cost, effort etc.
2	With three short-listed candidates remaining, selection may run beyond month 7 - what will be the impact for the remainder of the project? The final spend may exceed the estimate for this phase.	• Check the schedule for completion of this phase. • Review budget.
3	The issue in Spain may represent no more than a need to reschedule; however, the acquisitions will mean an expansion of the scope of the project - and therefore have cost and timescale implications.	• Expand the project to cater for the additional locations; this may have resource implications later on • Review budget implications.
4	Will the one month delay have any impact? What about the cost-benefit case and the benefits to be accrued by the business, which will start in month 7, not month 6?	• Revisit the benefit assumptions.
5	If support continues to run at this level, what are the implications for either resource levels or your ability to deliver against other planned commitments? (Indeed, is this why some things might be late already?)	• Revise assumptions if necessary. • Check impact of reduced developmant resource on future projects. • Check for any impact of 'non-productive' costs against the budget.
6	A success in terms of being able to accommodate additional work - but this wasn't in the strategic plan.	• The project needs to be retro-fitted into the plan. • Consider knock-on effects for support. • Are there any other projects that might be spawned from this initiative?
7	Loss of your senior database man could have a significant impact in terms of time taken to recruit and replace.	• Allow for this in any schedule if appropriate, e.g. the design phase of the ERP system.

Perhaps nothing too major here – but certainly enough to have some impact. Indeed, one could argue that the strategic plan has been 'compromised' by events, and could no longer be considered current – though this would be extreme.

The message must be to update, expand and verify. By undertaking the kind of actions indicated, you can be sure that your strategic plan remains a valid document – valid not only in the sense of its accuracy, but also in terms of the projections it enables you to make to the business of what and when you will be able to deliver. How many non-IT managers would not stop to consider the impact of the international acquisitions on an IT project already in motion? Under these circumstances, the strategic plan will continue to act as a solid platform upon which to plan, and provide a reliable guide for related activities such as budget planning. Indeed, get the maintenance of your strategic plan right, and the annual budgeting cycle ceases to be the nightmare it probably is today!

Consider the scenario once again. Two years into your five-year strategic plan and the first three major projects have all gone like clockwork; the fourth is well under way. You business colleagues have been hanging bunting in your honour for the last six months, and there's even talk that one day – and one day soon! – you might just make it to the board. Of course, the business is moving on too and flourishing, partly thanks to the splendidly consistent and reliable IT support it now enjoys – and you are keeping pace with these changes through your strategic plan, which is still valid and supported twenty-four months after you first wrote it. Happy? Content? You have every reason to be. And your laurels remain undented – after all, you've been far too busy to sit and rest!

Appendices

Appendix A
THE TEN COMMANDMENTS

Only promise what you know you can deliver.

A day well-spent in preparation, saves a week in execution.

Aim to delivery regularly, and aim to deliver 'real things'.

I.T. projects are ultimately business initiatives, and the responsibility for their success is a shared accountability.

An estimate is, in fact, an average. Do not forget this!

Failure to deliver even small things can erode confidence.

Nothing should be unmanaged.

Measure, measure, measure - but ensure that what your are measuring is meaningful.

Recognise the importance of internal communication.

Believe in the project. Believe in the strategy. Be enthusiastic about the future. Be clear about where people fit in.

Appendix B

A Strategic Plan

Below is a suggested contents template for a strategic plan. This is provided in outline format rather than with a specific structure including sample tables etc. to allow the Project Manager to customise the document to fit their own style and demands of their particular situation.

1. Introduction

    1.1. Preface

    1.2. Document Structure

    1.3. Document History

2. Management Summary

3. The Strategic Plan

    3.1. The Business Plan

    3.2. Strategic Terrain

    3.3. Strategic Expectations

    3.4. Plan Duration

    3.5. Scale

    3.6. Assumptions

    3.7. Constraints

    3.8. Strategy Ownership

    3.9. Quality Plan

4. Programmes and Projects

    4.1. Project "A"

        4.1.1.   Project Outline

        4.1.2.   Business Goal

        4.1.3.   Business Target

        4.1.4.   Business Owner

        4.1.5.   Business Contribution

        4.1.6.   System Proposal

        4.1.7.   Deliverables

        4.1.8.   Expected Business Gain

        4.1.9.   Timescale

Appendix C

A PROJECT DEFINITION REPORT

Below is a suggested contents template for a Project Initiation Report. This is provided in outline format rather than with a specific structure including sample tables etc. to allow the Project Manager to customise the document to fit their own style and demands of the project.

1. Project Overview

1.1. Outline
1.2. Business Background
1.3. Deliverables
1.4. Timescale
1.5. Cost
1.6. Benefits

2. Project Management

2.1. Authority
2.2. Escalation
2.3. Reporting
2.4. Quality Management
2.5. Risk Management
2.6. Issue Management
2.7. Project Performance Profile

3. Resourcing

3.1. Resourcing Plan
3.2. Key Players
3.3. Roles and Responsibilities

4. Project Influences

4.1. Assumptions
4.2. Constraints
4.3. Disaster Recovery
4.4. Validation

5. Delivery

6. Post-Delivery

Appendix D

BIBLIOGRAPHY

Baker S & K (1998) *The Complete Idiot's Guide to Project Management*, Alpha Books, New York

Brown M (1992) *Successful Project Management in a Week*, Hodder & Stoughton, London

Committee of Public Accounts (1999) *Improving the Delivery of Government IT Projects*, HMSO, London

Flowers S (1996) *Software Failure: Management Failure*, Wiley, Chichester

Hanks P, Ed. (1979) *Collins Dictionary of the English Language*, Collins, London & Glasgow

Lewis J (1997) *Fundamentals of Project Management*, Amacom, New York

Lientz B & Rea K (1999) *Breakthrough Technology Project Management*, Academic Press, San Diego

Peters T (1999) *The Project 50*, Random House, New York

Young T (1997) *30 Minutes to Plan a Project*, Kogan Page, London

Index